THE GREATEST COMEBACK EVER

ALSO BY JOE CONCHA

*Come On, Man! The Truth About Joe Biden's Terrible,
Horrible, No-Good, Very Bad Presidency*

*Progressively Worse: Why Today's Democrats
Ain't Your Daddy's Donkeys*

THE GREATEST COMEBACK EVER

Inside Trump's
Big Beautiful Campaign

JOE CONCHA

BROADSIDE BOOKS

HarperCollins books may be purchased for educational, business, or sales promotional use. For information, please email the Special Markets Department at SPsales@harpercollins.com.

Broadside Books™ and the Broadside logo are trademarks of HarperCollins Publishers.

FIRST EDITION

Designed by Michele Cameron

Library of Congress Cataloging-in-Publication Data

Names: Concha, Joe, author.
Title: The greatest comeback ever : inside Trump's big beautiful campaign / Joe Concha.
Description: New York, NY : Broadside Books, 2025.
Identifiers: LCCN 2024059648 (print) | LCCN 2024444474 (ebook) | ISBN 9780063435742 (hardcover) | ISBN 9780063435759 (ebook)
Subjects: LCSH: Presidents—United States—Election—2024. | Trump, Donald, 1946– | United States—Politics and government—2021–
Classification: LCC E919 .C66 2025 (print) | LCC E919 (ebook) | DDC 324.973/0934—dc23/eng/20250220
LC record available at https://lccn.loc.gov/2024059648
LC ebook record available at https://lccn.loc.gov/2024444474

25 26 27 28 29 LBC 5 4 3 2 1

CONTENTS

The Actual Joy Candidate | 1

How the Great Biden Cover-up Blew Up | 10

When We Saw Donald Trump Under Fire | 20

If JD Vance Is Weird, What Does That Make the Left? | 30

The RNC Hits Brew City, and the
Media Hits the... Green Screen | 37

Biden Steps—No, Stumbles—Down | 43

Kamalot: It Is a Silly Place | 51

The Midwest Dad That Wasn't | 68

Kamala Seinfeld: A Campaign About Nothing | 78

The "Positive" Side Sends Another Assassin | 90

The Endorsement Kamala Lacked: Forget *WaPo*,
It Was the Teamsters That Mattered | 96

The VP Debate Reveals Who's Actually Weird | 105

Media Blitz Causes Kamalacolypse | 113

The "Joy" Candidate Skips Comedy Night | 123

60 *Minutes* Sucks | 129

Trump Goes for the Bro Vote | 140

Live from Madison Square Garden | 149

Fry-Cook Trump Serves Up a Side of Fun | 157

Gold Standard Polls | 163

Sleepy Joe Jumps on the Trump Train | 170

Election Night | 181

The Delicious Aftermath | 190

The Billion-Dollar-Plus Bust | 209

The Trump Interview | 214

Epilogue | 223

Acknowledgments | 233

The Actual Joy Candidate

There is a good chance Trump loses the election. . . . And a good chance a judge in New York then sentences him to prison later this month.

—MEHDI HASAN

The left had tried everything. They indicted Donald Trump on obviously politicized charges. They tried to throw him in prison. They called him a fascist and a wannabe Hitler. They painted him as an angry and out-of-touch aristocrat.

But Donald Trump was like a member of the X-Men who gets stronger every time someone attacks him. Everything they did to try to take Trump down redounded to his favor.

A big part of the problem was simply this: the American people have eyes.

Confronted with the Chicken Little hysteria from the left, ordinary, reasonable people looked at Donald Trump, pumping his fists dancing to YMCA, working at McDonald's, making jokes about Hannibal Lecter, and hanging out with Joe Rogan.

Angry authoritarian? This guy?

Meanwhile, Joe Biden was drooling on national TV, and Kamala Harris, for all her "middle-class" platitudes, came off like a cold, cackling, consultant-constructed candidate.

A lot of people have asked where the moment was that it should have been obvious Donald Trump would win the 2024 election. The answer is simple: when the corrupt Biden administration indicted him. It turned him into an antiestablishment hero. And every subsequent attack would just do more to enhance that image.

The choice between corrupt bureaucrats and the change candidate who challenged them was obvious. Americans ignored the left's bullshit doomerism and pulled the lever for the real "joy" campaign. The only person who actually seemed like a meaningful change from the last four years.

I saw it coming. To be fair, who wouldn't? A little about me: Even on cold days, I like to hike. I can write and think and research, and the open air does the brain good. It's moments like these when my best ideas come to fruition.

This early 2024 hike didn't disappoint.

"Write a book on Trump's campaign. If he wins, it will be the greatest political comeback in American history," the *Field of Dreams* voice in my head told me.

"Write it, and they will come."

In retrospect, the fact you're reading this book is one of the better decisions I ever made outside of buying stock in Nvidia. But at the time, this book idea was still a risky proposition, simply for the unknown alone. Will Biden even make it to Election Day? Will Democrats throw Trump in jail? Will another pandemic be unleashed on us again and screw up another election?

I decided to bounce the idea off my editor at HarperCollins, a major publishing company responsible for my first two books. Said editor is a straight shooter and would tell me if it was a bad idea.

But he quickly agreed, noting that if I signed a deal and Trump was defeated or made an inmate, I could always pivot to a Plan B in terms of content. I had already hit the bestseller list twice for my previous two offerings during the Biden years, so they had confidence in my ability to write the kind of stuff readers found compelling regardless of the topic.

That same day, I reached out to Trump's closest aide on the trail,

Natalie Harp, and asked her if I could attend Trump's upcoming rally in my home and current state of New Jersey. I wanted to be behind the scenes for this book, and being backstage at a Trump rally would be a good start considering he doesn't come to New Jersey often and I had never experienced a rally.

Natalie, who, like Trump, apparently never sleeps, got back to me relatively quickly, and after sharing that the former president enjoyed my segments on Fox, she indicated the Trump communications team would be reaching out to coordinate my pass to the rally.

What I would discover on this trip was even more confirmation for my theory: Trump was the only choice for 2024 voters. Everything he did put the lie to the left's caricature of him. He was funny, normal, relatable, confident, and jovial despite the hail of knives rained in his direction by the Deep State's lawfare attacks.

About two days later, Karoline Leavitt, Trump's campaign spokesperson, whom you undoubtedly saw in interviews across the dial throughout 2024, emailed to say that transportation would be provided to take me to Trump's rally in Wildwood, New Jersey.

Needless to say, that offer was a relief, as my seventeen-year-old Acura was approaching the beginning of the end with 202,000 miles on it and an odd noise coming from the engine anytime I broke 60 on the highway, so having transportation provided was excellent news for the three-hour ride from North Jersey.

Then another email came.

Hi Joe,

President Trump would love for you to join the plane ride to Wildwood, NJ.

President Trump's scheduler will work with you to coordinate logistics.

Wait, what?

"Transportation provided" meant going to the rally on *Trump's plane*? Well, I thought to myself, this certainly beats the middle seat on JetBlue . . .

I was to meet Trump's team at a private terminal at New York's LaGuardia Airport. So on a sunny and cool Saturday afternoon on May 11, I found myself boarding Trump's jumbo jet to attend my first rally. And for whatever reason, my first thought upon being seated was . . . what food are they going to serve exactly? Would food be served at all? I had only had a yogurt around 7 a.m. that day and was starving.

My seat was in the back with a few other embedded reporters and the Secret Service. Shortly before takeoff, I was staring into space out the window when I heard that voice.

"Is that Joe Concha?"

I turned around to see a smiling Trump. It was a surreal moment in the sense that I had never met him before, yet he knew who I was from watching Fox, and obviously, I knew who he was. It felt like we already knew each other.

"Yes, sir. Thanks for the ride," I responded. "Big crowd expected today. I'm told we're [Fox News] going to carry it live."

"That's great. Appreciate everything you do on there. You're a good guy." Trump responded with a thumbs-up before being taken to his area in the front.

A few minutes later, I got my answer to the food-on-board question. Wendy's cheeseburgers. Tater tots. Fries. Coke. This was definitely a Trump plane. Apparently, a McDonald's wasn't close by, hence Wendy's. The fast food underlined something else about the campaign: as much as the left tried to pretend that Kamala Harris was the normal person in the race, it's impossible to imagine her naturally gravitating to the greasy goodness of a chain burger joint, like, you know, an ordinary person. And as Trump himself pointed out, it was impossible to imagine Biden even running a McDonald's, never mind the whole country.

From there, the plane flew directly over the New Jersey coastline.

I know some of you have this perception that my state is a polluted armpit of America with no redeeming qualities, but I was excited to see the familiar beach laid out before me. After all, I thought, this was the beach I spent my summers on. It's my favorite place on earth.

After doing a flyover of the rally site, which was already showing tens of thousands of supporters filling the sand below, we landed in Atlantic City, about forty-five minutes north of the rally. The motorcade was taking us south to Wildwood when something peculiar happened along the way on the Garden State Parkway.

The southbound highway, only two lanes at that point in the less populated part of the state, was blocked off for security reasons to make sure no cars could come up alongside Trump's SUV. I'm not sure what that radius was, but for a good thirty minutes, I didn't see one other car as we all occupied the right lane.

But then, out of nowhere, a civilian car, clearly not supposed to be there, came up alongside the motorcade and drove next to us for a good three or four minutes. It was a Honda Civic. There were two passengers.

What the hell was going on?

The car, thankfully, continued to slow up to allow the motorcade to pass it on the right before getting off at the next available exit; they can be spread out for miles. I was finally able to get a good look at those on board, and it was two older ladies who looked a bit confused as to the situation they accidentally landed in.

A false alarm, of course, but still . . . how exactly did the Golden Girls penetrate a motorcade of a former president?

Eventually we arrived at the small beach town of Wildwood. I hadn't been there since I was ten years old with my family. It consists of hotel after hotel on the water, multiple miniature golf courses, and a very large boardwalk and an amusement park complete with a water park. It is quintessential Jersey Shore, and absolutely Trump country. Wildwood's county, Cape May County, would go on to vote for Trump six months later by a 20-point margin.

Trump's entourage and the press, which included me, were housed in large tents behind the stage, complete with monitors with various networks on. A member of security eventually greeted me to take me out to a seat ahead of Trump's entrance. As I emerged onto the same runway the former president would use to walk out to my seat located in the first row, a chant began from the elevated bleachers behind the stage containing hundreds of people.

"Joe Con-CHA! Joe Con-CHA!"

Yeah, that really happened. And I had zero idea how to handle it, so I did the only thing a Jersey guy would do as a friendly gesture at the Jersey Shore. I pumped my first while yelling back: "You got that right!"

It was self-deprecating, I can assure you.

In another surreal twist, I was seated next to a Super Bowl MVP (Ottis Anderson) and Lawrence Taylor, the greatest defensive player in NFL history. Both were fans of Trump and were slated to join him onstage later.

Then the moment came for Trump to take the stage. I looked behind where I was seated, and there were people as far as I could see, and this was a *huge* beach.

But I noticed a few things that I can only characterize as odd: The amusement park behind where Trump was set to speak was still open. Rides that went high above the stage were still operating. And the boardwalk itself still had hundreds of people walking back and forth on it. Was that inside the security perimeter? Were these people screened? Also worth noting: a small plane was allowed to fly over the stage repeatedly. Carried a pro-Trump banner, sure. But why was any plane allowed to fly so close to the former president while he was speaking?

These ominous notes I had taken were something I never thought that I'd have to revisit down the road. But we all know what happened less than two months later in Butler, Pennsylvania.

Note: The agents stationed near Trump on the stage in Wildwood were constantly working, constantly watching. They seemed ready to act in a millisecond if needed. This account isn't an indictment of them. But things seemed a bit too lax in Wildwood that day. A military presence should have been felt on the outer areas of that event. I felt anything but.

Town officials put attendance that day at 100,000. It was the largest event in state history, and this was a political speech by a Republican in a state that Biden won by 16 points, no less.

"Thank you very much, Wildwood. Thank you," Trump said after extended chants of "Trump! Trump!" and "USA! USA!"

In addition to Trump as the normal-people candidate, he was also the one with a truly positive vision of America. Think about American flags, patriotism eagles, fireworks, hot dogs, spaceships—which candidate do you associate with those things? Not Kamala Harris, that's for sure. Only one candidate embodied this positive, forward-looking vision, Trump, as you can see from his opening riff that day in New Jersey.

"We love Wildwood. We've been here many times. We love this place. And there's nowhere else I'd rather be this beautiful evening. It is a nice one, right? Than right here on the Jersey Shore at the world-famous Wildwood Boardwalk. Great place, with thousands of proud, hardworking American patriots!"

The media always portrays Trump supporters as angry extremists. But my first rally gave me an entirely different takeaway: This felt more like an old Springsteen concert or your average NFL tailgate. And the merchandise is priceless. One woman I saw even had a custom sweatshirt that read, TRUMP: A PRESIDENT YOU CAN DEPEND ON, on the front and BIDEN: A PRESIDENT WITH DEPENDS on the back. Oof.

"He's incompetent," Trump later correctly said of Biden. "He's the worst president we've ever had. Other than that, he's doing quite a good job (laughter)." Trump's speech that day hit many familiar themes. He went heavy on illegal immigration and the economy. And, of course, there was this line about Hannibal Lecter that set off legacy media despite being a benign analogy/joke about those from insane asylums from other countries entering the U.S. illegally.

"An insane asylum is a mental institution on steroids. *Silence of the Lambs*. Has anyone ever seen *The Silence of the Lambs*?" Trump asked rhetorically, then riffed into his usual standup comedy style. "The late, great Hannibal Lecter is a wonderful man. He oftentimes would have a friend for dinner. Remember the last scene? Excuse me, I'm about to have a friend for dinner, and this poor doctor walked by. Hannibal Lecter, congratulations, the late great Hannibal Lecter."

Of course, the *Washington Post* reacted to that jokey line with trademark humorlessness. The headline was "Why Trump Keeps Talking About Fictional Serial Killer Hannibal Lecter."

And the subheadline: "Trump is the 'crypt keeper for the 1980s,' a Trump biographer said. Trump has mentioned Lecter while making baseless claims about immigrants."

First of all, they're not baseless, you hacks. And second, did someone surgically remove your funny bone? It's no wonder that the "Democracy Dies in Darkness" people don't know when their self-seriousness is blinding them to the real story.

Trump's remarks went on for nearly two hours that day. But in all my notes, this argument stood out the most because it made so much sense:

"I'm 'the politician,' if you can believe it. I hate to be called 'the politician.' I like 'I'm a businessman' much better, but I guess I'm a politician because we did great in 2016. We did much better in 2020, a lot better. We got millions more votes. So, I guess—and this time, and I will say this, the spirit that we have this time blows both of them away.

"You know why? Because you still like me, but you saw what the alternative is. The alternative, it's just—the alternative is not a good thing."

That's the thing: You had to *imagine* what a Hillary Clinton or Joe Biden presidency would be like when Trump ran in 2016 and 2020. But now that we have experienced the latter, many people appreciated the Trump years much more.

A *USA Today*/Suffolk University poll showed at the time that "51% of respondents said they now approve of Trump's job performance when he was president from 2017 to 2021, compared to 41% who said they approve of Biden's current job performance."

A major shift was happening not just nationally but in the Garden State. The electorate was angry across the nation overall. They wanted change. They wanted 2017–20 (pre-Covid) all over again and then some.

Panicked after seeing the poll numbers going the wrong way, President Biden directly challenged Donald Trump to a June debate in a scripted social media post with more edited jump cuts than a hyper TikTok video.

Trump being Trump, he immediately accepted the challenge that included every favorable condition to Biden. Trump was down for anything because that's what confidence looks like.

On June 27, I boarded a flight to Atlanta for that showdown between Biden and Trump.

It would be *the* most consequential debate in presidential campaign history.

How the Great Biden
Cover-up Blew Up

*I think people who might be thinking about voting for [Trump]
have to know that he can't last as president for four years with his
brain deteriorating at the rate it is.*

—NANCY PELOSI

It was a random February afternoon in 2024 when it happened.
Again.

"Helmut Kohl of Germany looked at me and said, 'What would
you say, Mr. President, if you picked up the London *Times* tomorrow
morning and learned that 1,000 people had broken down the doors . . .
of the British Parliament and killed some [people] on the way in [to]
deny the prime minister to take office?'"

That was then-president Biden talking about a conversation he apparently had with German chancellor Helmut Kohl at the G7 Summit back in 2021.

One problem: Kohl had already been dead for years. And he hadn't been in office for *over two decades*.

Before you say, well, everyone mixes up a date or has a senior moment now and again, the problem here is that this had become an ongoing thing with this president. Just a few days before that, he said this about the reaction out of France after his 2020 election victory: "And Mitterrand from Germany—I mean, from France—looked at me and said, 'You know, what—why—how long you back for?'" Biden mumbled.

Well, François Mitterrand was president of France, yes. But he left office in (checks notes) 1995 and died in 1996 . . . so in this case, Biden was only off by *a quarter of a century.*

Biden's brain turning to applesauce was happening more and more often, as well as his physical decline. The commander in chief was seen shaking hands with the air after speeches or wandering around trying to find where to exit a stage after doing these sort of events for more than fifty years. He forgot the names of his cabinet members on multiple occasions. He would stumble or fall outright going up the stairs of Air Force One so often that he switched from using the iconic public "tall" stairs on the plane to a more private, stable, short staircase. He fell off his bike in Delaware while approaching reporters on a perfectly flat surface. He fell at the graduation ceremony at the U.S. Air Force Academy after tripping over a rather large sandbag that Andrea Bocelli would have seen coming.

The left's first anti-Trump strategy may have been its stupidest. They tried to convince us that Joseph Robinette Biden was high-IQ—he was just too shy to reveal it in public.

At Fox News, we were seemingly alone among the major networks in calling all this for what it was: the mental and physical deterioration of the sitting president. The evidence was consistent. But over on MSNBC, D-list actresses like Mika Brzezinski were admonishing White House staffers for allowing Biden to fall instead.

"Do a better job because you can't have these video images of the president tripping or the president like going to wrong way. Because his age is going to be a factor. It makes me mad," she said on *Morning Joe* on July 12, 2023. Instead of pointing out that no world leader should need to be treated like a nursing home resident, she put the onus entirely on Biden's staff for not being good nurses.

"If you are managing a president's schedule and you're managing a president getting on and off stage, getting on and off planes, and yes, he's eighty. You need to be there for him. You need to make a pathway and you better make sure he doesn't fall on a sandbag. These are things that are going to hurt him played on a loop."

You see? It wasn't Biden's fault that he had turned into Chevy Chase doing his *Saturday Night Live* impression of President Gerald Ford, it was *everyone around him* who needed to be held accountable and do a better job.

I saw what you saw and what every lucid American was witnessing: an old man who couldn't handle being a Walmart greeter or golf starter at the local county course, let alone the commander in chief.

It was time for him to go.

But Biden wasn't going anywhere. He still believed he could beat Trump again, as did Dr. Jill, the first lady and fake doctor (my wife is an actual ER physician, and it drives her crazy when nondoctors call themselves doctors). He didn't seem aware the economy had gone to hell, especially regarding inflation and the cost of living. Crime was driving Americans out of cities large and small, fueled by Democrat mayors and district attorneys and illegal immigration, thereby driving Biden's numbers down further.

Illegal immigration was not only a national security crisis, with hundreds of terrorists on the FBI terror watch list coming in and more than 12 to 15 million illegals pouring over. This influx of people was imploding budgets for state and local governments across the country as they attempted to take care of them, to the tune of billions. Social services were cut, including to police, education, and sanitation. And those here legally, especially Latinos and Blacks, were getting increasingly pissed.

Throw in all the woke stuff around men competing against women in sports and kids getting sex changes without their parents' knowledge, and Biden was on the wrong side of every issue domestically.

On the other side of the aisle, Donald Trump had basically wrapped up the Republican nomination, crushing a popular governor in Ron DeSantis and a former popular governor in Nikki Haley. He was a freight train on the campaign trail and had an air of confidence that he was going back to the Oval Office in 2025. Why? Because he was on the right side of every issue and had the record to prove it.

The morning of the first (and as it turned out, only) debate between the two, my flight landed at Atlanta Hartsfield International Airport. The date was June 27, 2024. It was a typical Georgia day: 87 degrees, a bit humid, and a few showers in the afternoon.

For supporters of Donald Trump, there was confidence the forty-fifth president would destroy the forty-sixth president on the Georgia Tech campus that night. But there was also a worry that this thing could go sideways in a hurry with CNN hosting and Jake Tapper and Dana Bash—two staunchly anti-Trump moderators for the past eight years—running the show.

The scenario was an easy one to imagine: Trump was going to be interrupted. Fact-checked. He would lose his temper, like he did in the first debate against Biden in 2020, when moderator Chris Wallace was Goose to Biden's Maverick that night in teaming up on Trump, who was suffering from Covid at the time.

If Biden performed even remotely well, the media would declare him the winner while insisting Trump was unfit and (insert various adjectives here). Biden would ride that wave of (manufactured) momentum all the way to the Democratic National Convention. And if the media did the job they were told to do by Joe's people, the rest of the campaign up until November 5 would be a referendum on Trump not on policy, but as a threat to a democracy that *must* be stopped.

And you knew many in the press would do as they were told. Check out MSNBC's Joe Scarborough, not long before the debate, piously telling anyone who dared to question Biden's cognitive health to go fuck themselves.

"Start your tape right now because I'm about to tell you the truth," Scarborough exclaimed, patently unhinged. "And fuck you if you can't handle the truth. This version of Biden, intellectually, analytically, is the best Biden ever. Not a close second. And I've known him for years. . . . If it weren't the truth, I wouldn't say it."

He actually said that with a straight face. Because this Joe isn't a journalist or even a cable news host. He's the kind of cheesy actor you see at 3 a.m. on Skinamax.

Meanwhile, Biden had a rough go leading up to the debate at the G7 in Italy, where he appeared to wander off during a group photo with world leaders. He also confused Italy and France. And then there were off-teleprompter remarks like these that give one the impression the elevator is no longer going to the penthouse anymore. Here is one example, verbatim, regarding his "accomplishments" on the economy:

> And there's a lot of other... For example, the idea that we're... in terms of taxes that they refuse to... for example, we, I was able to balance the budget and pass everything from the global warming bill anyway, I was able to cut by $1.7 billion in the first two years the deficit that we are, were accumulating and because I was able to say to that the fifty-five corporations in America that made forty-four hundred billion dollars or forty billion dollars, four hundred billion dollars, that they pay zero in tax, zero.

A sane observer would see what was happening and conclude the president was a few fries short of a Happy Meal. But the media wasn't having it, of course, and insisted that any videos of Biden saying and doing old-man things were simply "cheap fakes" driven by "right-wing media."

Right on cue, enter hacktivist Brian Stelter, who *never* disappoints. "We've been worried for years about AI deepfakes that computer-generated images are going to trick people into believing something that's totally false. Cheap fakes are a little bit simpler," the former host of the hilariously named *Reliable Sources* argued. "They're cheap. They're just distorted out-of-context videos chopped up in certain ways, constructed in certain ways. That's what we're seeing."

CNN would go on to rehire Stelter a few weeks later. To quote Commodus in *Gladiator*: "It vexes me. I'm terribly vexed."

Taking no chances, Team Biden tucked the president away before the debate with Trump at Camp David to prepare for *six days*. And the geniuses handling him thought it was a swell idea to have sixteen *people* in the room to prepare him. Was Biden's CPU, which is the equivalent of a '72 engine in a Dodge Dart, equipped to handle all this information being fed into his internal hard drive?

Per the *New York Times* before the debate, it was also revealed that "the preparations . . . never started before 11 a.m. and Mr. Biden was given time for an afternoon nap each day, according to a person familiar with the process."

A nap. That's nice. And we all start our workdays at 11 a.m., right?

But no matter. This wasn't about *winning* the debate.

All Scranton Joe had to do was survive.

Nine p.m. ET. Atlanta. The debate begins. And like an old Tyson fight in the 1980s, you knew Biden was going down quickly. *Way* more quickly than anyone expected.

His mouth was agape while Trump spoke when he wasn't looking off in another direction. The president looked dazed and confused. Seventy million people were watching live across the country. All of them had been told by legacy media that Biden, at least behind the scenes, had the brainpower of Stephen Hawking and the physical speed of Herschel Walker. He was solving quadratic equations and explaining how the flux capacitor worked and why it needed plutonium and 1.21 jigawatts. Many of them had believed it, either because they knee-jerk believed people who pontificated on TV and had a fancy degree, or because they weren't paying attention.

No one could believe the secret-genius Biden theory after that performance.

So how bad was it that night? Here's a quote from Biden on a question on Medicare.

"Making sure we make every single solitary person eligible for what I've been able to do with COVID, excuse me, with, umm, dealing with everything we had to deal with," Biden said as his voice trailed off and his operating system ran out of memory. His brain was crashing in real time. "Look, we finally beat Medicare."

"He beat Medicare, all right," Trump deadpanned in response. "Beat it into the ground."

At another point, Biden laughably claimed the border is much more secure under him than Trump. "It's better than when he left office. And I'm going to continue to move until we get the total ban on the [mumbling again, then long pause]—the total initiative relative to what we're going to do with more Border Patrol and more asylum officers."

"I really don't know what he said," Trump deadpanned. "And I don't think he does either." That was Trump's demeanor throughout the evening. He was completely in command. He never lost his cool. And he obviously understood that he needed to be disciplined while allowing Biden to sink himself.

The headlines afterward were brutal from a shocked media. Even they couldn't smother this raging dumpster fire.

CNN: "Biden's Disastrous Debate Pitches His Reelection Bid into Crisis"
Time: "Inside Biden's Debate Disaster and the Scramble to Quell Democratic Panic"
USA Today: "'Sense of Shock': Democrats Melt Down over Joe Biden's Debate Disaster"

The *New York Times*, which hasn't endorsed a Republican presidential candidate since Dwight D. Eisenhower (meaning they endorsed Humphrey, McGovern, Carter twice, Mondale, Dukakis, Gore, and Kerry as part of its sterling record), went to DEFCON 1, with all of its top columnists going on record demanding Biden step aside as if a memo went out, with its editorial board also stating the same.

Sorry, assholes . . . you don't get to play dumb on this one. You saw exactly what we all saw *before* that debate and called anyone who called it out a purveyor of cheap fakes and fearmongering.

Remember this headline? "How Misleading Videos Are Trailing

Biden as He Battles Age Doubts." With the subheadline: "A flurry of recent clips, many of them edited or lacking context, laid bare a major challenge for the president as he tries to persuade voters he has the energy for a second term."

Take a bow, *Times.* These are called receipts.

"It was the biggest train wreck of any presidential candidate ever," observed Fox News' Sean Hannity in the postdebate coverage on Fox. "When he wasn't speaking, he was staring out like an empty vessel."

Joy Reid on MSNBC, perhaps the most pro-Biden, anti-Trump person on cable news, said this: "My phone never really stopped buzzing throughout. The universal reaction was . . . approaching panic!"

Van Jones on CNN: "He didn't do well at all . . . there's time for this party to figure out a different way forward if he will allow us to do that."

The Drudge Report, which has become vehemently anti-Trump and is practically unrecognizable these days, had these as its siren headlines:

OPERATION: REPLACE BIDEN
DEMS SCRAMBLE WITH 130 DAYS TO GO!
DEBATE CATASTROPHE

Then there was *Politico,* with the simplest sum-up: "Biden Is Toast."

This was the biggest one-night earthquake we've seen in American politics since, like, ever. Biden was already the underdog, but this cemented him losing at least *400 electoral votes* per his own internal polling. An ex-Obama speechwriter only revealed that tidbit after the election, shivving his boss's old embarrassing vice president for the last time. It would have been a blowout.

The Senate? Gone.

Winning back the House? Please.

But Biden is the grandpa who still wants to drive the car to the store. He *ain't* giving up the keys. And Jill *really* loved being first lady. So along with Hunter and career hangers-on like the swampy Ron

Klain, a cone of protection was formed around the tired old man. He wasn't going anywhere. Even with those internal polling results, his team criticized Kamala to reporters, saying she couldn't win, and that Joe was abso-frickin'-lutely the best possible candidate to win.

But the cat was out of the bag. After the debate, no one could deny it. Those Democrats looking to win in November quickly ran to X to make their feelings known. The loudest voices were the ones who felt the most in danger in the upcoming election.

(Vulnerable) Then-Senator Sherrod Brown (D-OH): "I agree with the many Ohioans who have reached out to me. At this critical time, our full attention must return to these important issues. I think the president should end his campaign."

(Vulnerable) Then-Senator Jon Tester (D-MN): "While I appreciate his commitment to public service and our country, I believe President Biden should not seek reelection to another term."

(Still reprehensible) Representative Adam Schiff (D-CA): "While the choice to withdraw from the campaign is President Biden's alone, I believe it is time for him to pass the torch. And in doing so, secure his legacy of leadership by allowing us to defeat Donald Trump in the upcoming election."

When I provided my analysis on the debate for Fox afterward, I said the following: "Joe Biden is done. He is not going to be the Democratic nominee. There isn't going to be another debate [between Trump and Biden] in September. And look, we've been talking about this for many, many months, if not years: as far as his cognitive ability, as far as his mental acuity, as far as his ability to speak outside of a teleprompter, it simply does not exist anymore.

"So now the question is, who replaces Joe Biden at the top of the Democratic ticket? Because this isn't a matter of if, but when."

To make matters worse for Team Blue, their lawfare efforts against Trump were falling apart. Less than one week after the debate, the U.S. Supreme Court ruled 6–3 that Donald Trump had "absolute immunity" as president when conducting official acts. From a macro perspective, that meant almost all legal experts believed there was no way that Jack Smith's election interference case against Trump—the most serious and highest-profile prosecution he faced—was going to be tried before Election Day.

But as June became July and the Independence Day weekend took politics off the radar for many Americans for several days, Biden appeared to have survived the initial wave of calls to pass the torch. What did all of this mean for Trump? Of course, we know what it ultimately meant: he would run against Kamala Harris instead of Joe Biden. But in a broader, strategic sense, it meant the left couldn't attack his intelligence in any way without looking like hypocritical idiots. Donald Trump became the presumptive high-IQ candidate. They'd need to find a new manner of attack.

On July 8, here's what a defiant Biden said as he attempted to go on offense. And it was beyond abhorrent, which was hardly a surprise, as I learned in writing my first book, *Come On, Man! The Truth About Joe Biden's Terrible, Horrible, No-Good, Very Bad Presidency*, which chronicled this guy and the way he has conducted himself his entire life. He's truly an abhorrent person.

"I have one job, and that's to beat Donald Trump. I'm absolutely certain I'm the best person to be able to do that. So, we're done talking about the debate," Biden said before ominously adding, "It's time to put Trump in a bull's-eye."

Five days later, Donald Trump boarded his plane for a rally at a large field in the Rust Belt town of Butler, Pennsylvania, located about thirty-five miles north of Pittsburgh.

But hours earlier that day, a drone with a camera had also taken off to survey the grounds where the former president was set to speak.

A would-be assassin wanted to find the best place to have a clear shot at the former president.

And, boy, did he ever find it . . .

When We Saw
Donald Trump Under Fire

We simply cannot expect that someone [like Trump], who is facing this number of criminal trials, and, quite frankly, the conduct that underlies those charges, can be a viable fall election candidate against Joe Biden.

—CHRIS CHRISTIE, AUGUST 2023

It was a sunny and especially hot Saturday afternoon in July when I ventured into New York City to Fox News headquarters to cohost *The Big Weekend Show*. My executive producer had mentioned in her correspondences with the team that a Trump rally could run into our 7 p.m. ET live show, and our focus would initially be to discuss it after taking it live in its entirety.

As I entered the greenroom in Studio M, Trump was just taking the stage. As I always try to do, I settled in to see if we would hear anything differently from Trump now just two weeks removed from a disciplined debate performance. He had a solid lead after the debate, something he never had in 2016 and 2020 from a polling perspective, so I was curious if Trump would continue being the contented battler and perhaps make some new policy proposals in continuing to go on the offensive.

Calls were growing for Biden to step aside as the polls got worse, but from his perspective, he thought he simply had a bad night, he was still within striking distance, and who wants to have a legacy of being a quitter?

Meanwhile, Trump wasn't worried about the old man at all. His demeanor was decidedly different than it was in 2020: He was the challenger now, there was no Covid hanging over the entire election, and Biden's record on the economy, crime, and the border was patently horrific. There was also a growing nostalgia among Americans for the Trump years after they had experienced the Biden ones.

This allowed Trump to be more of the freewheeling, happy warrior on the campaign trail than in the previous cycle. So despite temperatures in the nineties at the start of his Butler speech, out walked Trump in a full suit and red MAGA hat.

Cohosting with me that night were Katie Pavlich, Jason Chaffetz, and Miranda Devine, three of the more affable and knowledgeable people you'll meet in this business. At 6:13 p.m., Miranda was still back in makeup while Jason and Katie were heading back that way as well. I was in front of one of the two large TVs in Studio M.

Then it happened.

One gunshot. Then two. Three.

Pop-pop-pop-pop-pop-pop-pop-pop . . .

Screams from the crowd.

And Trump grabbing his ear like something just stung him before hitting the deck.

"Holy shit! Holy shit! I think Trump got shot!" I yelled as Katie and Jason came running back in.

"It was either his neck or his ear," I explained while still in a state of shock, my eyes glued to the TV.

Seeing that happen live on national television was one of the most jarring things I had ever experienced. For the next minute or so, it was hard to tell exactly what was happening. Trump was covered by Secret Service agents, some of whom I had met during the Wildwood rally two months earlier.

To everyone's relief, Trump was eventually brought to his feet by the agents and you could see he could move of his own volition. It was clear he wasn't badly hurt. But before the former president was escorted off the stage to the nearby motorcade, one of the most badass things you'll ever see occurred: Trump craned his neck over the agents to be clearly seen by the crowd, and pumped his fist in the air with blood splattered across his face.

While he had no audio, the words he shouted were clear. "Fight! Fight! Fight!"

He was going to be okay.

Without taking my eyes off the screen, I said to no one in particular, "He just won the election, didn't he?"

I almost felt guilty for seeing things through a political prism in that moment, but since it was clear Trump was only grazed by a bullet, it felt safe to say. And I have a feeling I wasn't alone in that sentiment. He seemed invulnerable, strong, and shockingly courageous in the face of a close call with history.

The Big Weekend Show was rightly preempted as expected, of course, and I went home. My kids, ages eight and ten at the time, had seen the attempt on Trump's life played on a loop many times at that point and asked me why anyone would try to do such a thing.

"There are bad people in the world" was the only thing I could muster up. "The important thing is Mr. Trump is going to be fine."

"I don't want you going to any more rallies," my daughter said.

I didn't have the heart at the time to tell her I was headed for Milwaukee in a few days for the Republican National Convention. So my wife and I landed on Daddy simply having a "business trip" to go on, which was technically true.

Trump's iconic bravery was sadly not the only outcome of the rally. The assassin, Thomas Crooks, just twenty years old, was killed right after getting off eight shots, but one of those shots killed Corey Comperatore, a local volunteer fireman, husband, and father. Corey had leapt to shield his family after the shots rang out, and died protecting them. Two other attendees, David Dutch and James Copenhaver, were also hit but thankfully survived.

On my end, what had started out as shock and relief had quickly given way to anger and curiosity as reports came in regarding the attempt and we started to understand how unprepared the Secret Service had been for an assassin.

WTF #1: We quickly found out that more Secret Service resources were assigned to Jill Biden attending a small event indoors in Pittsburgh than those assigned to protect Trump at an outdoor rally in a field with tens of thousands of people in attendance. It's an absolute joke that Jill Biden was given priority over one of the most threatened public figures on the entire planet, especially since it was revealed that Iran had an active plot to assassinate him as revenge for Trump's order to take out General Qasem Soleimani, an Iranian terrorist responsible for the deaths of hundreds of American troops in Iraq. Soleimani was killed via a U.S. drone strike at Baghdad International Airport in January 2020.

WTF #2: A roof less than 150 yards from Trump's position onstage was not secured by the Secret Service or local law enforcement despite providing a perfect line of sight to the potential target. How could that *possibly* be overlooked? Why wasn't there anyone on the roof to begin with? With a scope, an open 150-yard shot with a line of sight is the equivalent of a two-foot putt.

"Multiple Secret Service personnel mistakenly assessed these line-of-sight risks to the former President as acceptable, leading to inadequate elimination," a Secret Service report later explained. If that's the case, whoever deemed this risk "acceptable" should be fired. But more on that in a moment.

WTF #3: How did the Secret Service determine that a building *that* close *with* a line of sight to Trump was outside the inner perimeter? An AR-15 has an effective range of 400–500 yards.

WTF #4: Crooks was identified by a local SWAT sniper over ninety minutes before the shooting. The sniper called him a person of interest, spotting him hanging around fifty yards from the exit. Crooks was spotted again around an hour before Trump took the stage. Crooks was walking around with a rangefinder. Not illegal, but suspicious as hell? Surely you'd send up an alert to someone else on the team. Right? *Right?* But there was no communication between the local SWAT and the Secret Service about these findings. Despite the potential active threat, someone decided to send Trump onstage anyway. *Trump should have been secured backstage or removed from the grounds altogether until the threat was found and contained.*

WTF #5: Photos were taken of Crooks on the roof before he opened fire. Oh, that's nice. People around the rally were pointing at him, trying to get cops involved. In videos, you can hear people say, "Someone's on top of the roof. Look!" Is there anyone who didn't notice this guy?

WTF #6: Law enforcement snipers were *in* the building (which does absolutely nothing) below Crooks. Secret Service director Kimberly Cheatle later explained the snipers couldn't be on the roof because it was slanted (utter bullshit).

WTF #7: How again did a twenty-year-old kid outflank the Secret Service and law enforcement by hiding a rifle behind an air conditioner at the building, and how did not one person discover it?

WTF #8: A local police officer attempted to climb onto the roof but quickly came down after Crooks turned and pointed a rifle at him. Why wasn't Trump rushed off the stage then?

WTF #9: Before the attempt, a Secret Service countersniper team didn't get a radio that local law had left for them, thereby leading to a breakdown in communication. *Why?*

"These breakdowns in communication contributed significantly to the mission failure, leaving much of the law enforcement personnel performing protective operations, including former President Trump's protective detail, unaware of key information leading up to the attempted assassination," the report said.

WTF #10: Why, to this day, as you read this, wasn't *one person* fired over this?

There are other WTFs, but you get the point. As I said on the air in August, we're well past simple incompetence and well into asking a legitimate question:

Was Trump never supposed to leave that stage?

Crooks, it turns out, got off the shot that *should* have killed Trump.

But thanks to, of all things, a chart outlining explosive growth in illegal immigration under Biden-Harris, Trump had to turn his head at a hard-right angle to see it. The sharp turn meant the bullet grazed his ear instead of his head, which likely would have killed him instantly.

"That chart that I was going over saved my life," Trump told Dr. Ronny Jackson that night. Jackson served as Obama's and Trump's White House physician before successfully running for a House seat in Texas.

"The border patrol saved my life," Trump said to Jackson. "I was going over that border patrol chart. . . . If I hadn't pointed at that chart and turned my head to look at it, that bullet would have hit me right in the head."

What's amazing and awe-inspiring—and I don't ever use those words to describe anyone other than Michael Jordan or Tom Brady—is what Trump was thinking about as the Secret Service stood him up. He could have been thinking of himself or his family. He could have gotten the hell out of there just in case there was a second shooter.

Instead, his first thought was to let his supporters know, and let the country and the world know, that he was going to be okay and to keep on fighting.

Fight!

Fight!

Fight!

It reminded me of an underappreciated scene in the movie *Rocky Balboa*, which effectively served as *Rocky VI*. At this point, the Italian Stallion has been retired for a long time but still has "some stuff in his belly" he wants to get out. In other words, he wants to return to boxing. I feel the same way about football. After we won our state championship in high school (Let's go, Valley!), I never played another down in pads again. It's hard to walk away from something you love doing.

Rocky decides he wants back in and wants to teach his adult son, who objects to his decision to get back in the ring, about never giving up. Rocky Jr. was plodding along in life without much self-confidence while still being in the shadow of his legendary father.

Search YouTube for this clip if you get a chance.

"The world ain't all sunshine and rainbows. It's a very mean and nasty place, and I don't care how tough you are, it will beat you to your knees and keep you there permanently if you let it," Balboa explains. "You, me, or nobody is gonna hit as hard as life. But it ain't about how hard you hit, it's about how hard you can get hit and keep moving forward. How much you can take and keep moving forward. That's how winning is done!

"Now if you know what you're worth, then go out and get what you're worth," he continues, his voice rising. "But ya gotta be willing to take the hits, and not pointing fingers saying you ain't where you wanna be because of him, or her, or anybody! Cowards do that and that ain't you!"

That's Trump. He gets knocked down and keeps moving forward. It could be ninety-four felony counts, two impeachments, accusations of Russian collusion, a constant bombardment of hostile media coverage . . . or a friggin' bullet.

And the man just keeps moving forward.

But some in our media couldn't help themselves, with some profound morons asking if a bullet even hit Trump at all. It's such a ridiculous question, but it was actually broached on the insane asylum that is MSNBC.

Enter former Republican National Committee chair Michael Steele, who demanded proof Trump was actually shot.

"It's been three days—going on four—since this horrific event occurred," Steele told Ari Melber and Jen Psaki. "A person lost their life, and two have been severely injured. And yet we've not received a medical report from the hospital, nor have we received a medical report from the campaign or from the Trump Organization about the extent of the damage to his ear.

"If he was shot by a high-caliber bullet, there should probably be very little ear there. And so, we'd like to know that. Is there cosmetic surgery involved? What is the prognosis for recovery? Were there stitches? What is the extent and nature of the damage to his ear?"

Remember, this is the same person who never once questioned anything about Joe Biden's health, and now he wants a full report on whether Trump got shot? Where did the blood on Trump's face come from exactly?

"Was it caused by a bullet as opposed to—as some reports from those on the scene, other reporters—saying that it was actually shards of glass from the teleprompter itself, not the bullet?" Steele added. "So there are a lot of questions around that ear."

How delusional do you have to become to even question this happened? Steele opened the possibility that the bullet may have hit Trump's teleprompter, and glass may have caught his ear instead. But fact-checks quickly debunked that conspiracy theory because the prompters remained fully intact.

"The assertion that glass, not a bullet, caused the injury is undercut by the fact that photographs show no damage to the teleprompters allegedly hit to produce the broken glass, by a *New York Times* photograph capturing a bullet passing by Trump's ear, and by the fact that Trump later stated, on Truth Social, that a bullet had, in fact, pierced his ear," reads the fact-check by Snopes.

"Trump's description of his wound matches photographs of his ear after he was hit, prior to being removed from stage," it adds while showing a photograph of Trump's wounded ear upon being escorted off the stage.

Not to be outdone, Melber accused Trump of using the bandage on the ear as a prop.

No really . . .

"This is also showmanship by a politician known for his mastery of what they call unscripted reality TV. Taking this supremely visible seat in the VIP box with his new running mate and party leaders and a longtime TV personality, Tucker Carlson, up there as well last night," Melber said on the first night of the Republican National Convention, which took place just two days after Trump was shot.

"Here's how the *New York Times* put it," the host continued in quoting an equally insulting *New York Times* article. "On the first night of this convention, Trump was his own biggest prop. He entered the VIP box, a large white bandage on his injured right ear, the result of a close call on Saturday with a would-be assassin's bullet. A reminder of mortality, a badge of survival—it was a blank rectangle on which the crowd could read what it wished, and that made it the most potent placard in the hall.

"That's fair," Melber concluded while adding his own commentary. "A placard for delegates to fill in, an image for political mobilization, a spectacle for this candidate who we know is—by his own admission— obsessed with assorted spectacles."

Again, this was forty-eight hours after an assassination attempt on a former president, and this was the crap these twisted individuals served up.

The morning after that comment, I told Melber to go to hell on *Fox & Friends First*. It went viral. Normally that's not my goal, but an exception had to be made in this case. It was infuriating to listen to.

From there most of the media memory-holed everything about the assassination attempt. Democrats, in the span of a week, went back to the rhetoric that inspires unhinged people to try to "save democracy" by taking out Trump with a bullet instead of a ballot.

An NBC News poll found that a majority of voters (54 percent) believe that "extreme political rhetoric used by some in the media and by political leaders was an important contributor" to the attempt on Trump's life. That's an insanely high number.

We'll never know what Crooks's motive was. We'll never know if he was working with someone or some entity.

Secret Service director Kim Cheatle was subpoenaed to appear before the House Oversight Committee eight days after the attempt. She refused to answer basic questions around how Crooks was able to get onto that roof, citing an ongoing investigation.

"I'm not going to get into specifics of the day. There was a plan in place to provide overwatch, and we are still looking into responsibilities," she lamely explained.

"You're full of shit today!" Representative Nancy Mace (R-SC) exclaimed while accusing Cheatle of being "completely dishonest" with the committee. "We have asked you repeatedly to answer our questions."

Cheatle would concede that the security breakdown was "the most significant operational failure of the Secret Service in decades."

"I accept responsibility for this tragedy," Cheatle said. But when Mace asked if she would draft a resignation letter, she refused.

Even Representative Alexandria Ocasio-Cortez, aka AOC (D-NY), had heard enough after Cheatle said a report would be completed for review in *two months*.

"The idea that a report will be finalized in sixty days, let alone prior to any actionable decisions that would be made, is simply not acceptable," Ocasio-Cortez said. "It has been ten days since an assassination attempt on a former president of the United States, regardless of party. There need to be answers."

Cheatle would resign not long after that hearing. She should have been fired first.

A press looking for the truth would continue to dig for answers here, but within just a few days, it was back to hammering Trump. Americans watched all of this unfold and saw an administration that rushed to prosecute Trump and dragged its feet on investigating an assassination attempt on him. They were nuking their own credibility as a legitimate government. Meanwhile, Trump led from the front . . . When under fire, for all he knew, he made sure to reassure the people around him that he was bloodied but unbowed.

This leadership quality would show up again when he announced his running mate. It was still unclear heading into the Republican National Convention in Milwaukee two days after the attempt on Trump's life who he was going to choose to be his running mate. There were certainly plenty of fine options.

My preference was Glenn Youngkin. My second choice was Marco Rubio.

Turns out I was way off on this one.

If JD Vance Is Weird,
What Does That Make the Left?

I don't see how [Trump] wins.

—JIM CRAMER, CNBC

J ames David Vance may go down as one of the greatest success stories of the twenty-first century. And that's not hyperbole.

Think about it: If the Trump 2.0 presidency is a success, Vance is all but certain to be your 2028 Republican nominee. He'll have Trump's blessing and, therefore, that of the growing coalition that is the MAGA voting base, which now includes a growing number of working-class union rank-and-file, Blacks, Latinos, and younger voters. And it's just hard to see anyone perceived as outside that MAGA world somehow beating a sitting vice president if the approval numbers for the administration are solid.

If inflation is lowered, wages are raised, gas prices go down thanks to energy independence, if the border is secure, and if the world is a more peaceful place, JD wins not only the nomination in 2028 but also the presidency.

Because ask yourself this: What can Democrats run on after four years of Biden-Harris and a decided push to the fringe on policy and cultural issues?

So if JD is president and has a historic eight years building off the Trump momentum, he will have accomplished all of this before reaching even his mid-fifties. The sky's the limit from there.

Naturally, with the announcement of his pick, the left lost its mind. JD Vance, a self-made success, a husband and father, a veteran. This guy was labeled "weird" and "creepy as hell."

The date was July 15, 2024. Two days earlier, Donald Trump nearly lost his life by a millimeter in Butler, Pennsylvania. But here he was, less than forty-eight hours later, announcing to the world that he had chosen his vice president.

"After lengthy deliberation and thought, and considering the tremendous talents of many others, I have decided that the person best suited to assume the position of Vice President of the United States is Senator J.D. Vance of the Great State of Ohio," Trump posted on Truth Social.

Full transparency: my reaction was surprise. Vance's name was always in the running, sure, but I wasn't sold on what he brought to the ticket at the time. He had underperformed two years earlier in winning a Senate seat in Ohio: Republican governor Mike DeWine had won reelection to the tune of 25 points in the same election cycle, while Vance won by less than 6. Why did he run 19 points behind the governor?

My choice, as previously mentioned, was Governor Glenn Youngkin of Virginia. He was like Trump in that he jumped into politics after being successful in the private sector and therefore wasn't part of the swamp. He was seen as an underdog against the Clinton machine (in Youngkin's case, against Clinton royalty Terry McAuliffe, a former Virginia governor who was the clear favorite to win that gubernatorial race in 2021). But Youngkin, a folksy optimist who ran against woke educational and Covid policy, ended up winning relatively comfortably in a state Biden took by double digits in 2020.

So my thought process was a fairly straightforward one: choose Youngkin, who had just a *34 percent disapproval* rating in Virginia, and Trump could end the night early by taking the state, thereby rendering the Blue Wall useless to the Democratic nominee (it was Biden at the time of the selection) if holding the Sunbelt. But Trump chose Vance instead, which reportedly was the choice all along for Trump's sons, Don Jr. and Eric, who pushed their dad hard on selecting him.

I wasn't the only one baffled by JD, but the left was positively gleeful at the pick, assuming he'd be a millstone on a campaign that had had its problems. They should have realized that the bestselling author of a memoir showing the strength of the American Dream could never be that. We all know JD's story by now: He grew up in an abusive household in the Ohio Rust Belt and was raised by a drug-addicted mother who was married and divorced several times. The environment was anything but stable, especially for a boy without a father after his dad walked out on the family when he was a toddler. JD was eventually placed in the care of his grandparents, who as union Democrats were responsible for his upbringing.

Upon graduating from high school, Vance joined the U.S. Marines, where his duties included serving as a public affairs officer, which meant dealing with the media. After his Marine Corps service, he graduated from Ohio State University in just two and a half years, a testament to his intelligence, before getting a degree from Yale Law School.

Vance proceeded to become the bestselling author of *Hillbilly Elegy* and shined during media tours for the book and the movie promotional tours that followed. In 2022, he became a United States senator at age thirty-eight.

Out of the gate, things were bumpy for JD, as would be expected of anyone tethered to Trump in this toxic media environment. The "weird" label appeared to be sticking, although no objective person could point to why that was. Then there was the silly controversy about an offhand joke Vance made about childless cat ladies on Tucker Carlson's show in 2021.

His argument was that Alexandria Ocasio-Cortez and others were screaming about climate change as the reason they don't want to bring children into this world: If we were all going to die anyway on this hellscape of a planet, with rising sea levels, no polar ice caps, droughts, and heat, why bother having kids?

"There's scientific consensus that the lives of children are going to be very difficult. And it does lead young people to have a legitimate question: Is it okay to still have children?" she asked in 2019.

Remember, this is the same person who declared that humans only had twelve years left before climate change made this world uninhabitable. So, by that count, since the comment was made in 2018, we've only got five years left at this point. Nice knowing ya . . .

Vance heard the AOC argument and summed it up thus with Tucker: "We are effectively run in this country via the Democrats, via our corporate oligarchs, by a bunch of childless cat ladies who are miserable at their own lives and the choices that they've made, and so they want to make the rest of the country miserable too."

Not one person or politician blinked an eye when he said that at the time. Because there's nothing controversial about it.

According to a Nielsen Scarborough survey, "single-person households with cats are almost two times more likely to be female."

According to the latest census, 21.9 million women in the U.S. between ages 20 and 39 had not given birth in 2022, a historic low.

A population where fewer children are born can have a very real impact because the trend is undeniable and profoundly disturbing from an economic and cultural perspective. Overall, 44 percent of those between 18 and 49 years old say it's unlikely they'll ever have children, an all-time high.

Regardless of the reason, birth rates have fallen sharply in the past fifteen years. How sharply? The most recent Census Bureau data shows that the U.S. population grew just 0.4 percent in 2022, which is a slight increase from 2021, but worse than every other year over the past *one hundred years*.

Overall, U.S. fertility rates are at record lows. For context, according to the National Center for Health Statistics, in 1960 the average woman had given birth to more than three children. By 2018 that number had dropped down to just one child. Fertility has especially declined in recent years, with the average number of children born to a woman going from 2.12 in 2007 to 1.65 in 2021.

The problem is even more profound in dying cities like San Francisco, where there are more dogs than children, where the latter make up just *13 percent* of the population.

The reason all of this matters is simple: Baby boomers are now at or exceeding retirement age. And as more leave the workforce, the need for younger workers is more crucial to keep the economy moving.

According to the Census Bureau, one in four Americans will be older than sixty-five by the year 2060. And having fewer babies consequently means there are fewer working-age people to support the surge in retiring and aging baby boomers. Fewer workers to replace older workers means less output. Less output results in a lower standard of living. And it will be the final nail in the solvency of the Social Security coffin if less money is being put into its already-severely-drained system.

So was JD correct? To quote another VP candidate, "You betcha."

The numbers are the numbers, and if any journalist worth their salt had explored the argument in any serious way instead of sharing their liberal emotions on the matter, we might have had an honest discussion.

Instead, this was the result:

CNN: It's Not Just "Cat Ladies": JD Vance Has a History of Disparaging People Without Kids
ABC News: JD Vance Slammed for "Childless Cat Ladies" Comment
Washington Post: JD Vance's Repeated Digs at Childless Women Is Worse than You Thought

Polls began to emerge not long after showing Vance with the lowest favorability numbers of any of the candidates.

"I certainly wish that I had said it differently," Vance later said of the controversy in an interview with the *New York Times*. "What I was definitely trying to illustrate ultimately in a very inarticulate way is that I do think that our country has become almost pathologically anti-child.

"But I think that is a bizarre way of thinking about the future. Not to have kids because of concerns over climate change? I think the most bizarre thing is our leadership, who encourages young women, and frankly, young men, to think about it that way," he continued. "If your political philosophy is saying, 'Don't do that because of concerns over climate change?' Yeah, I think that's a really, really crazy way to think about the world."

Amen.

But Trump didn't lose faith in his selection. And instead of using the Democrat strategy of hiding its candidates, Vance was given the green light to do *more* interviews on networks and with publications that exist only to make Republicans uncomfortable.

But that was the thing: Vance never appeared uncomfortable while on CNN or doing the Sunday morning shows back-to-back-to-back on ABC, NBC, and CBS.

How's this for a stat?

In the month of August, Trump and Vance did 34 interviews total. Harris-Walz: 1.

My favorite moment came during JD's appearance with the impossibly condescending Martha Raddatz. You remember Martha . . . she is the ABC News "journalist" who appeared to cry on the air after Trump won in 2016.

Anyway, check out this exchange regarding violent Venezuelan gangs in the country illegally who took over whole apartment complexes in Aurora, Colorado. Vance broached it during the interview with Raddatz after Trump called it an invasion during a campaign stop in Aurora to highlight the crisis.

"Senator Vance, I'm going to stop you because I know exactly what happened. *I'm going to stop you,*" a defiant Raddatz declared. "The incidents were limited to a handful of apartment complexes—apartment complexes and the mayor said our dedicated police officers have acted on those concerns. A handful of problems."

Vance responded just about as perfectly as one could ask with mockery and common sense.

"Only, Martha, do you hear yourself?" he asked. "Only a *handful* of apartment complexes in America were taken over by Venezuelan gangs, and Donald Trump is the problem and not Kamala Harris's open border?

"Americans are so fed up with what's going on, and they have every right to be. And I find this exchange, Martha, sort of interesting, because you seem to be more focused with nitpicking everything that Donald Trump has said rather than acknowledging that apartment complexes in the United States of America are being taken over by violent gangs."

"Okay. Let's just—let's just—let's just end that with, they did not invade or take over the city as Donald Trump said," a flustered and defeated Raddatz said, looking for an escape hatch.

"A few apartment complexes, no big deal," Vance chuckled.

Brilliant.

Unlike Kamala and the goofy Tim Walz (who came up with the whole "weird" attack), the *more* Vance spoke, especially in hostile territory, the more people got to know him, respect him, *like* him.

In September, according to YouGov, just 35 percent of voters had a favorable opinion of JD. By November 9 postelection, that number shot up to 44 percent favorable.

So with the selection of his VP solidifying the ticket, I joined Trump and Vance at the Republican National Convention in Milwaukee. It would mark the first time I ever covered a presidential convention in person and not just by watching from afar.

The atmosphere inside the arena was as happy and confident as one could possibly imagine.

But another huge plot twist was about to turn this race upside down just seventy-two hours after Trump accepted the nomination for a third time.

The RNC Hits Brew City, and the Media Hits the . . . Green Screen

He's definitely going to lose. You can just feel it. I promise you.
Don't worry. Don't think about it. I don't think about it.
—BILL MAHER, OCTOBER 2024

On July 15, 2024, the Republican National Convention kicked off in Milwaukee, in the key swing state of Wisconsin. Trump took the state in 2016 and was leading in 2020 on Election Night until mail-in ballots magically handed the state to Joe Biden by 20,000 votes.

But going into the RNC, Trump was up big in the cheesehead state, leading by 6 points in the polling average over Biden. He was just shot in the ear two days earlier. Meanwhile, Biden was on a media blitz trying to convince people he could still do the job for the next four years, but he was flailing even in friendly interviews. Everything was going Trump's way heading into the convention. You could feel the optimism, an air of inevitability, from supporters who packed the Fiserv Forum, the home of the NBA's Bucks, each day and night that week.

Naturally, you wouldn't have known that from the mainstream media, who would go on to demonstrate how disconnected they were from regular voters over the course of the convention, from literally refusing to show up to rolling their eyes at uplifting American films.

As I entered the arena for the first time, it became quite apparent that 99.9 percent of those in attendance watched Fox News and Fox Business, based on the number of selfies I was asked to take. I half joke with my kids that Daddy is just a D-list cable news celebrity, but it's basically true: I don't have my own show, but I do get a ton of airtime from early morning to late evening. And the thing about Fox viewers is this: they're extremely loyal. Many will share that they literally have the network turned on all day, and when they're not watching, they're at least listening like a radio in the background. I know this to be true, with some relatives sharing the same exact sentiment.

Fox News and Fox Business were broadcasting out of what appeared to be a luxury suite in the mezzanine section of the arena, as was every other major network except MSNBC. Not sure you knew this, but that garbage "news channel" covered the convention from New York, with Rachel Maddow, Nicolle Wallace, Joy Reid, Jen Psaki, and others sitting on a set at 30 Rock but with an LED screen background that made it appear they were sitting on the convention floor.

No, really.

"Is Maddow in Milwaukee? No, That's an LED Screen on MSNBC," was the *New York Times* headline.

"If news organizations don't represent where they are clearly, then how is the audience to have faith and confidence in the actual content of the reporting?" asked respected media analyst Frank Sesno in an interview with the paper.

Even CNN finally got a chance to sneer at another network not named Fox, with Jake Tapper beginning an interview with Marco Rubio thus: "Thank you, guys, and you're actually here live," Tapper snarked. "We're live as opposed to some other networks that just have a big LED, who shall remain nameless."

That's how bad it was for MSNBC. Network brass knew that no Republican would even entertain the thought of being interviewed by the likes of Maddow or Reid or Psaki, so sending these "anchors" to Milwaukee was pointless. But the fact they tried to manipulate viewers into believing they were there is why so few trust the media as a whole.

Joe Scarborough and Mika Brzezinski have been doing the same thing for years on *Morning Joe*. The duo likes to spend their winters down in Florida, all while portraying themselves as Washington insiders. So oftentimes on their program, we would see Joe and Mika on a set with the Capitol or other D.C. monuments in the background. Their panels joined them in these situations from 30 Rock in Manhattan but also would have Washington backdrops. The whole thing is the essence of the married hosts of the show: phony.

Getting back to the Republican convention before I really go off on a tangent, I was waiting to join Martha MacCallum for a hit from the Fox suite when something happened that I never could have predicted. Someone bear-hugged me from behind. I felt my bones cracking. It was like a human vise was squeezing me. Then I heard that voice:

"I LOVE YOUR WORK, BROTHER. WATCH YOU ALL THE TIME," he bellowed directly into my ear.

Yep. It was Hulk Hogan. At seventy-one, he still was completely ripped. He was there to speak on the final night of the convention before the former president. This was so typical of the Trump coalition: while the Democratic convention had elites like Oprah Winfrey, Mindy Kaling, and Kerry Washington, the GOP had the Hulkster, Dana White, Kid Rock, and Dennis Quaid.

I shared with Hulk that it was perfect timing that we had met because the night before I left for Milwaukee, my son and I watched *Rocky III*. That movie has a hilarious scene with Hulk as the fictional professional wrestler "Thunder Lips," who pulverizes Rocky for the better part of five minutes before Rocky has Paulie cut off his gloves to fight back and score a draw before the charity fight is mercifully stopped. Amazingly, that movie came out more than forty years ago.

With some time to kill in between interviews, I went to our makeshift greenroom to bang out a column for the *New York Post*. It was there that another familiar voice was directed my way.

"Hey, Joe Concha, when are you getting your own show?" asked a smiling Dennis Quaid, while extending his hand.

This guy is somehow seventy years old. He was there to promote his new movie, *Reagan*, where he masterfully portrays the popular fortieth president, who was easily the greatest president of the twentieth century, stewarding a strong economy while taking down the Soviet Union without firing a shot.

Being the dork I am, I went full fanboy on Dennis, reeling off a series of movies that I enjoyed off his long résumé: *The Right Stuff*, *The Parent Trap* (my daughter introduced me to that one), *Any Given Sunday*, *Great Balls of Fire*, *Wyatt Earp* . . . the list goes back to the 1970s with *Breaking Away*.

"What was your favorite movie to do?" I asked him.

"*Reagan*," he replied immediately. He called it the challenge of his life because Ronald Reagan, while being a great public communicator, was a very private person who was impenetrable to everyone except Nancy.

Much of the movie follows Ronald Reagan behind the scenes, dating back to his days as a heartthrob lifeguard (girls would act like they were drowning just to be "rescued' out of the water by him in one amusing scene). It also covers his broken marriage with Jane Wyman; his time as a successful, then struggling actor; how he met Nancy; his obsession with studying the Soviets and communism; and his jump from heading the Screen Actors Guild to governor of California to eventually the presidency. But what was really great about the movie was how it pushed back against the propaganda view of the Cold War—it clearly casts the Soviets as the bad guys, not misunderstood intellectuals who made a few bad choices on their way to famine and dictatorship.

Reagan would go on to be panned by liberal critics, receiving just an 18 percent positive score out of 100 on Rotten Tomatoes.

"The faithful for whom 'Reagan' was made aren't likely to see that it's a hagiography as rosy and shallow as anything in a Kremlin May Day parade. As pop-culture propaganda—popaganda, if you will—the movie's strictly for true believers. As history, it's worthless," Ty Burr of the *Washington Post* angrily wrote.

"You may have suspected that this MAGA-tinged hagiography

would be absolute trash, but it turns out you didn't think low enough," critic Nick Schager wrote in the trashy Daily Beast.

But once again, this is where elitist movie critics, who are mostly based in New York and Hollywood, are completely disconnected from their readers: When asking the *Reagan* audience for their reviews on Rotten Tomatoes, the film received a 98 percent positive score, one of the highest of all time. For context, classics like *Forrest Gump* received a 95 percent positive score for audiences, while 2023's Best Picture, *Everything Everywhere All At Once*, received a 79 percent positive score.

Reagan would go on to finish third at the box office on its opening week despite being on a fraction of the screens as big-budget movies like *Alien: Romulus* and *Deadpool & Wolverine*, all while doubling box-office expectations in bringing in $10 million on Labor Day weekend.

The 2024 Republican National Convention ended up being one big party. Trump's acceptance speech was incredible to witness—and it was a miracle he was still alive. The most poignant moment came when Trump kissed the helmet of slain firefighter Corey Comperatore, who was shot and killed in Butler with bullets meant for Trump, during his address.

Even MSNBC couldn't find a way to criticize this tribute, could they?

Well, guess again. Meet Symone Sanders, who worked for Vice President Kamala Harris as a spokeswoman and senior adviser before abruptly resigning in December 2021 to go to MSNBC, where she was handed her own show.

"I was sickened by them using him as a prop, his firefighter jacket, and then they spelled the man's name wrong," Sanders raged. "This is not, you know, Chicago fire. How come they got their names on the back of the jacket like who are you fooling? But then they put the name on it and they spelled it wrong. I was just kinda like if we gonna—if we gonna do props like, let's at least get it right."

Oh, about that "controversy" of Comperatore's name being spelled wrong on his firefighter jacket seen onstage. The name was indeed wrong—it was spelled Compertore, minus an *a*. But it turns out neither Trump's team nor Republican staff misspelled the name; it was the Butler Fire Department that originally did years ago. But Comperatore didn't care and didn't want to ask the department to spend any additional money on having another jacket made, so he kept it. Sanders could have done a quick Google search in the ninety minutes she had to check on this before spouting out misinformation on the air, but she didn't. She never apologized either. MSNBC execs offered no reprimand, of course, because they are petrified of their own "talent."

The convention officially ended after Trump's speech. After doing a *Fox Nation* special with Pete Hegseth, David Webb, and James Freeman that lasted until 1 a.m. and joining *Fox & Friends First* at 4:30 a.m. central time, I hitched a ride to Chicago with some veteran *F&F* producers and Lawrence Jones, along with his service dog, Nala, who seemingly is always by the side of the tireless *Fox & Friends* cohost.

The whole convention had done even more to demonstrate how out-of-touch the media was with ordinary Americans. They preferred to put the outside world up on a green screen instead of actually interacting with the masses. Is it any wonder they were going to miss the story of the greatest comeback ever?

Part of it, of course, was that they were still carrying water for the incumbent, the secret genius.

The date was July 19. My first family vacation was set to begin in two days on a Sunday. But the sitting president was going to make sure there would be no rest for anyone in the news business for the foreseeable future.

A political earthquake was about to erupt.

Biden Steps—
No, Stumbles—Down

If Trump is on the ballot next year, the GOP is looking at a wipe-out of epic proportions up and down the ballot.

—SCOTT MOREFIELD, TOWNHALL

July 21, 2024. Cape May, New Jersey

The day had finally arrived: The Concha family's first vacation of the year! We usually spent a week on Long Beach Island, since we have many friends there, but instead we decided to try something different and go farther south on the Jersey Shore and check out the sights and sounds of Exit 0 off the Garden State Parkway.

After unpacking and loading up the wagon with chairs, shovels, boogie boards, and books, it was time to finally relax on the beach. I had worked a ton to this point in the year, with the insane news cycle always keeping us even busier than usual in an election year. I decided I wasn't going to look at my phone much over the next few days and left it in the hotel room to truly get away.

And just as my toes hit the sand, my wife gave me the news from an alert on her phone.

Joe Biden just dropped out of the race.

"Who do you think they'll replace him with?" Jean asked.

"Kamala," I replied before adding something along these lines:

"Not sure what other option they have. They could nominate someone at the convention, I suppose, like Gavin Newsom or Gretchen Whitmer, but I just don't see that happening. They'll piss off more than a few people if they just leapfrog the woman next in line."

At the time, I was unaware that the Biden-Harris campaign war chest was nontransferable when I made that observation. There were, in fact, $350 million reasons why Kamala had to be handed the nomination. The money was hers to spend now and no one else's. The Democrats, contrary to their messaging that they were the true party of the poor, ultimately think elections are won off of billionaire funding. They rake in millions of—over a billion!—dollars and spend like it's 1789, and Versailles needs a new wing.

I went back to the hotel to get my phone just in case Fox wanted me to join. It's not so much that I'm that special, of course, but that the bookers for every show know I have a professional home studio and could jump on within a few minutes of being contacted. But this time there was no home studio, just my cell phone. And when I got back to the room, I had three missed calls and a ton of text messages from work and friends all about Biden.

"Hi Joe. Can you join now to discuss Biden dropping out?" wrote one booker.

"Just checking in again. I booked your home studio. Are you available?" she wrote again.

"??????:)," she followed as I was checking the other messages.

I usually get back to these hardworking folks very fast, hence the "Dude! Where are you?" messages that came in after being away from my phone for even thirty minutes. I called back and said I could join, but it would have to be from the hotel room on my cell through what is essentially a Zoom call.

It was at that moment that I realized my backup jacket, shirt, and tie that I keep for these situations was in the back of my Honda CRV (which had just replaced the old Acura mentioned earlier, which finally broke down for good) back at home 170 miles north. For space purposes with all the packing, we took my wife's larger Honda Pilot instead, therefore no jacket, no shirt, no tie. The only decent thing I had to wear for this hit (interview) was an old button-down, off-white Banana Republic shirt I think I purchased in 2004. I did have a polo, but it was a bright yellow Savannah Bananas shirt. I opted for the Banana Republic offering. It was a summer Sunday in the midafternoon, so viewers likely wouldn't be thinking, What the hell is he wearing?

At this point after many almost starts and stops, the bookers had found many of our biggest people on Fox to discuss Biden dropping out, so I was relieved of my duties, at least for that afternoon. During the rest of the vacation, however, I did join several shows from the hotel ballroom through my phone, which was perched on top of a candle lantern to create a steady, eye-level shot. As for my fashion, I learned one very simple truth about the Cape May/Wildwood area: there are *zero* men's stores. I had to drive thirty minutes inland to find a Marshalls, and it had no jackets or sport coats but did have exactly one white button-down shirt in my size and one pinkish-and-blue tie that I wore that week and never touched again out of respect to the viewers at home.

Okay, enough about me and inside-baseball stuff; let's get back to Biden. After the announcement that he was stepping aside, there was no press conference scheduled, no questions from reporters allowed. This was par for the course for this joke of a leader, who answered fewer questions than any president in our lifetime. But this wasn't just any day. Biden had done something we haven't seen since Lyndon Baines Johnson: a sitting president saying he won't seek reelection.

In LBJ's case, he had stepped aside in 1968 for two reasons: his health was deteriorating (he died four years after leaving office) and the escalating Vietnam War and protests had worn him down. He made the decision before anyone had noticed these problems, though. The combination of his big-government initiatives and his spin of bad Vietnam news had made him unpopular on both the right and the left. His popularity was in the tank. LBJ knew when it was time to step aside, but the move still shocked almost everyone in the country.

In Biden's case, his health—both mental and physical—was also deteriorating, but he wouldn't admit it. He spoke to George Stephanopoulos of ABC News shortly before he exited as he was trying to save his candidacy in the wake of that horrific performance in the debate against Trump.

"Do you dispute that there have been more lapses, especially in the last several months?" Stephanopoulos asked.

"Can I run the one hundred in ten flat? No. But I'm still in good shape," Biden replied.

Unconvinced, Stephanopoulos followed: "Are you more frail?"

"No," Biden insisted.

"Do you have the mental and physical capacity to do it for another four years?" Stephanopoulos also asked.

"I believe so. I wouldn't be runnin' if I didn't think I did," Biden said. "Look, I'm runnin' again because I think I understand best what has to be done to take this nation to a completely new—new level. We're on our way. We're on our way."

On our way, all right . . . on our way to being a third-world nation. Ultimately, inflation, crime, the open border, wars overseas, and Afghanistan will be Biden's legacy, along with being a walking corpse before being bullied out of office by his own party. Worst president since the late Jimmy Carter. It's not even close. Maybe the worst *ever*.

Biden's bid to hang on to the nomination failed twenty-four days after the debate. During those three and a half weeks, he saw his biggest supporters turn against him. It got to the point that he lost George Clooney! The *Ocean's Eleven* star wrote an op-ed in the *New York Times* begging Biden to get out.

"It's devastating to say it, but the Joe Biden I was with three weeks ago at the fund-raiser was not the Joe 'big F-ing deal' Biden of 2010," Clooney wrote on July 10. "He wasn't even the Joe Biden of 2020. He was the same man we all witnessed at the debate."

Gee, thanks, George. I guess your original plan was to *not* disclose what you saw behind the scenes at that Hollywood fundraiser in mid-June, all while hoping that the jacked-up State of the Union version of Biden would show up to that debate instead. And only after the entire country was made privy to the true state of his mental fitness did you decide to come forward. You sure are a big patriotic hero. But give Clooney some credit: at least he did come forward, unlike late-night coward Jimmy Kimmel, who hosted the fundraiser that night.

Truth be told, Biden never should have run again in the first place. He should have dropped out months before to allow the party to have a proper vetting of candidates through the public's eyes via an extended primary process. The left's first strategy—pretend Joe Biden is secretly Albert Einstein—was now to pretend he was a hero for dropping out of a race he obviously couldn't have won, and too late for someone to take over who actually could. Some hero!

If that occurred, it is almost a guarantee that Kamala Harris wouldn't have won the nomination. She was attached to Biden on everything voters hated about the state of the country. And she's simply one of the worst candidates to ever seek high office.

Despite his pudding brain, I think Biden understood who and what Kamala is and knew he had a better chance to defeat Trump than she did. He likely saw her the way that many of us do, as a power-hungry individual who will say *anything* to get elected. That's exactly what she did in 2019 when she believed running to the left of Bernie Sanders was a winning strategy. Through his octogenarian brain fog he remembered Kamala implying he was a white supremacist during the 2019 campaign, and supporting the women who said he'd made them uncomfortable by doing his usual hair-sniffing routine. But Kamala had turned on a dime when Biden wasn't an opponent but a potential employer.

Surely no one else would remember Kamala as an unreliable flip-flopper. Right? *Right?*

A few days later when Harris became the presumptive nominee after Nancy Pelosi ordered other Democrats to get in line and stand behind her, her campaign had their first big decision to make: What media outlet would she give her first interview to after being selected to be at the top of the ticket? *60 Minutes*? *Meet the Press*? A sit-down with Jake Tapper? Would she be bold and do an interview with Bret Baier on Fox News to make her case to a huge audience?

Nope.

Instead she ran to . . . *RuPaul's Drag Race.*

Not kidding.

"Each day, we are seeing our rights and freedoms under attack, including the right of everyone to be who they are, love who they love, openly and with pride," Harris crooned, sitting next to RuPaul while clearly reading a teleprompter. "So as we fight back against these attacks, let's all remember, no one is alone."

The trans issue would go on to be a top issue in swing states. Polls at the time showed that about 70 percent of voters were against biological men competing against biological women, for example. Naturally, with her innate sense for promptly finding a woodchipper to dive into, Kamala decided that attempting to appeal first to the other 30 percent was a smart idea, instead of leaning toward the moderate center and affirming their blatantly logical concerns about a radical left-wing agenda.

Shortly after she was doing the drag thing, on August 1, Trump's strength versus Harris's weakness was on display once again in Chicago during the National Black Association of Journalists convention. Right out of the gate, the Republican nominee was treated with outright hostility by Rachel Scott of ABC News.

"I want to start by addressing the elephant in the room, sir. A lot of people did not think it was appropriate for you to be here today," she began. "You've pushed false claims about some of your rivals, to Nikki Haley, to former president Barack Obama, saying that they were not born in the United States, which is not true. You've told four congresswomen of color—who are American citizens—to go back to where they came from. You've used words like 'animal' and 'rabid' to describe Black district attorneys. You've attacked Black journalists, calling them a 'loser,' saying the questions they asked are stupid and racist. You've had dinner with a white supremacist at your Mar-a-Lago resort. So, my question, sir, now that you're asking Black supporters to vote for you, why should Black voters trust you, after you've used language like that?"

"I don't think I've ever been asked a question in such a horrible manner, first question. You don't even say, 'Hello, how are you?' Are you with ABC? Because I think they're a fake news network, a terrible network. I think it's disgraceful that I came here in good spirit," Trump rightly replied.

"I don't know why you would do something like that. Let me go a step further: I was invited here, and I was told my opponent—whether it was [Joe] Biden or Kamala—I was told my opponent was going to be here. It turned out my opponent isn't here. You invited me under false pretense," he continued. "And then you are half an hour late. Just so we understand, I have too much respect for you to be late. They couldn't get their equipment working or something was wrong. I think it's a very nasty question."

Scott's nasty question would be a preview of the way Trump would be treated by ABC News at a debate with Kamala the following month. And by the way, the charges were beyond disingenuous, especially the parts about Trump attacking Black journalists and Black district attorneys. Trump attacks everybody who attacks him. Is Jim Acosta or Joe Scarborough or Maggie Haberman Black? Are prosecutors like Jack Smith or judges like Arthur Engoron Black? Trump goes after anyone he perceives to be a hostile opponent. Skin color has zero to do with it.

But at this NABJ event, despite the "questions" from Scott, he hammered home his points around illegal immigration impacting minorities through social services being drastically cut regarding sanitation, education, and police to help pay to support those in the country illegally. Trump also underscored the cruel tax that inflation is to all communities regardless of color.

Meanwhile, Harris decided to blow off the event. Why? Because her people knew that if she ever had to take questions from an objective, prepared co-moderator like Fox's Harris Faulkner, who was also there that day, it would be utterly disastrous to her campaign. She simply did not have the ability to think or speak extemporaneously. And her policy positions on U.S. taxpayers paying for sex changes for illegals or opposing all offshore drilling or supporting late-term abortion were simply indefensible in a general election.

So the first goal of her campaign was in place: avoid any substantive questions at all costs, and try to eke out a win without ever being held to account.

Not that Kamala was going to spend her time alone. The strategy was to hide from the public, but become best friends with the people who are supposed to inform that public. Moving forward, Kamala would still need the support of that group that represents almost every Democrat's biggest ally.

Enter the stenographers who call themselves journalists, and who in this election cycle brought bias and outright activism to a whole new low . . . proving that rock bottom indeed has a basement.

Kamalot: It Is a Silly Place

Donald Trump will not win the general election. . . . He will not win a general election. There will be a female president of the United States. It will either be me or it will be Kamala Harris.
— NIKKI HALEY

Kamala Harris was the most unpopular vice president in history. That's not an opinion, it's what the polls told us.

That's quite a feat considering Dick Cheney used to hold that distinction, and he's the veep who literally shot another guy in the face on a hunting trip while in office. Dick's also the guy who lied us into war in Iraq on the false premise of weapons of mass destruction, resulting in the loss of thousands of American military servicemen and women with countless maimed and permanently injured.

But when Joe Biden was shown the door by the axis that is Pelosi, Obama, and Schumer, there were few options for the Democrat Party. Should it hold a lightning primary and find a candidate that way in a span of less than a month before the party's convention in August? Should it just decide the thing on the convention floor in Chicago?

Or should they turn to its current VP, the aforementioned most unpopular in polling history, and anoint her?

In the end, *always* follow the money. And that's where the answer to this question lay. Three hundred fifty million dollars of it was waiting to be used in the Biden-Harris campaign war chest. So the only choice was Kamala . . . horrible record, bad campaigner, impossible to work for, nails-on-a-chalkboard cackles and all. And before you say, well, shouldn't, you know . . . *voters* have a say in this decision instead of installing a candidate in what one could call the most undemocratic way possible?

Fuhgeddaboudit . . .

Yep, this was 2016 all over again. Just like with Hillary, the Democrat Party elites were going to crown another unpopular candidate. Except this time they wouldn't have to use the kind of shenanigans they did when making absolutely sure Bernie Sanders didn't sniff that nomination in 2016. Remember that? We found out per WikiLeaks dumps at the time that the Democratic National Committee harbored utter disdain for Bernie and favoritism toward Hillary. The leaks were so damaging that the DNC's chairwoman at the time, Debbie Wasserman Schultz, was forced to resign *during* the convention. Couldn't happen to a sweeter gal. It just goes to show that Democrats running their party like a secretive cabal of wealthy puppet masters calling the shots from above goes back a long time. It's no wonder they're out of touch. It would immediately become a meme that Kamala referred to her "middle-class family" upbringing because no one actually saw her as connected to the workers of America.

But regardless of being handed the nomination without a single vote and therefore no vetting, Kamala was still going to need major help taking on Donald Trump, who was already leading big in the polls and fresh off his bravura response to an assassination attempt that had played out on live national television. So the campaign turned to the one ally the Democrat Party could always most rely on: the legacy media.

It's hard to say anything new about the corruption of the American left-wing media, but the 2024 campaign really did demonstrate how cloistered and blinkered they are as a class. As much as they talked about "checking your privilege" and tried to paint the right as the party of the rich, this election showed that it was the Harris-supporting media that were the true elites. They didn't check their own privilege!

So there's the question: When did the media get so out of touch? Folks, I've been studying and covering this stuff going back to the 2004 campaign, when *60 Minutes* and Dan Rather tried to alter the outcome of that race after dropping a farcical report on George W. Bush's National Guard service just before Election Day that year. Legacy media always serves at the pleasure of the Democrat Party; they're just more overt about it now.

If you recall, the crux of Rather's report relied on documents that were quickly proven false after the story was broadcast since the font used on said documents didn't exist in 1972, when they were allegedly written that put Bush's service into question. Rather, displaying the hubris of the defeated has always maintained that the documents were "fake but accurate."

That's when the slow slide of media trust began. In 1981, 81 percent of the country had a positive opinion of Walter Cronkite upon his retirement as anchor of *The CBS Evening News*, according to Gallup. Rather succeeded Walter, but before he was fired for the fake documents scandal, just *21 percent* told Gallup they believed him "all or most of the time," or a 60 point drop.

Rather was fired not long after. In 2024, he rambles on X about the horror of Trump while having the balls to lecture us on media ethics.

Things got worse in 2008 during Barack Obama's coronation as America's first Black president. Bernie Goldberg sums it all up in his book on the media's posture during the race between John McCain and Obama in his book, *A Slobbering Love Affair: The True (And Pathetic) Story of the Torrid Romance Between Barack Obama and the Mainstream Media*. Obama was barely vetted and hardly criticized, and mild-mannered war hero McCain was portrayed as a sexist curmudgeon and a racist.

Yes, *that* John McCain. And how, again, was he racist? Because he compared Obama to Britney Spears in a campaign ad in an attempt to portray him as a sizzle-over-steak media celebration rather than someone with actual substance.

You know, like Kamala in 2024 . . .

Check out this take in *Politico* at the time in August 2008.

"But it wasn't just the Britney-Paris ad that channeled voters' inner Orval Faubus. McCain's follow-up video joked that the star-struck press corps had anointed him 'The One,' a man that could not only 'do no wrong' but could also probably, with powers bestowed by the media, part the Red Sea," the August 2016 piece reads.

"Cue the clip of Charlton Heston in *The Ten Commandments*. Here, too, was the specter of racism," it continues.

"When you see this Charlton Heston ad, 'The One,' that's code for, 'He's uppity; he ought to stay in his place,'" political consultant David Gergen said on ABC's *This Week* at the time. "It's the subtext of this campaign. Everybody knows that."

Yup. That's basically how it went. Evoke Britney and Charlton Heston as Moses, and you're actually attempting to appeal to Republican voters, who are really all just closet racists. The insanity is so much like the coverage we just witnessed in 2024 that it's scary.

It somehow got even worse in 2012 when the milquetoast Mitt Romney was portrayed as a dog-abusing reincarnation of a sexist, racist version of Gordon Gekko. That year, the coverage was astonishingly and embarrassingly biased. As an example, the Pew Research Center found that of the 51 stories MSNBC did on Obama in the campaign's final week, *all* 51 were positive, while *all* 68 stories it did on Romney were negative.

And it wasn't just MSNBC, but almost everywhere. According to Pew Research, "From October 29 to November 5, [2012], positive stories about Obama in mainstream media outlets outnumbered negative ones by 10 percentage points. On the other hand, negative stories about the GOP nominee Mitt Romney outweighed positive stories by 17 points." That's a 27-point delta.

In a close race, a 27-point difference in media coverage (and remember, this is well before Twitter and podcasts became dominant forces) can make the difference in a close race. Obama, despite a horrible economy, unemployment still high (7.9 percent), and soaring deficits, won reelection with some tight victories in swing states like Ohio and Florida (yes, Ohio and Florida used to be considered swing states). Mission accomplished.

So after seeing not only what happened in 2008, and 2012, and the way Trump was covered in 2016 and 2020 (see: with utter disdain, dishonesty, and hostility), Team Kamala summoned their stenographers in the press to portray the new Democrat nominee as a completely different person and candidate than she was during her failed 2019 campaign, which saw her drop out before her own home-state primary in California, and well before the first votes were cast in Iowa. *She was that bad.*

For starters, she has authenticity issues. Likability issues. People forget that when Kamala launched her first presidential campaign, she was hailed as the female version of Obama.

It was January 2019, and twenty thousand people showed up to her launch rally in Oakland, California. She was the first major candidate to announce, and many in the media had her as the front-runner. Her stock only grew after the first primary debate a few months later, when she executed a rehearsed line accusing future boss Joe Biden of racism due to his old position on school busing and segregation.

"It was hurtful to hear you talk about the reputations of two United States senators who built their reputations and career on the segregation of race in this country," Harris said while looking directly at Biden. "And it was not only that—you also worked with them to oppose busing."

Kamala went on to recall her experience as "a little girl in California" who was bused as a second-class citizen to assimilate public schools in her county.

"And that little girl was me. So I will tell you that on this subject, it cannot be an intellectual debate among Democrats. We have to take it seriously. We have to act swiftly," she added.

Jill Biden never forgot about Kamala accusing her husband of being a racist. But more on that later. And it's tremendous.

Taking the bait, the media swooned. Enter Van Jones after that debate in 2019.

"A star was born tonight," Jones declared. "This is a masterful performance. She completely dominated the stage. And most importantly, she would kick Donald Trump's butt, and she proved it tonight. If you had any doubt that you could nominate a woman that would take Donald Trump to the woodshed, she just took it away from you."

Okay, that is beyond funny to read now.

As summer became fall in 2019, Kamala began speaking more in interviews, which turned out to be a mistake (sound familiar?) because she was saying some pretty radical shit that turned off many voters.

Consider this doozy of a comment: "It is important that transgender individuals who rely on the state for care receive the treatment they need, which includes access to treatment associated with gender transition," she declared at the time. "That's why, as attorney general, I pushed the California Department of Corrections and Rehabilitation to provide gender transition surgery to state inmates."

Gah. And a few weeks later, after polls showed her trailing (checks notes) *Andrew Yang* in the California primary and with the money quickly drying up (sound familiar?), Kamala bowed out.

The Trump campaign would later use this exact sound bite on U.S. taxpayer dollars paying for sex changes for inmates five years later. It would go on to be one of the most effective political ads in history.

But more on that ad later.

Months later, after Democrats including Pete Buttigieg and Elizabeth Warren and Amy Klobuchar stepped aside one by one before Super Tuesday to allow Joe Biden to become the de facto nominee, the former vice president announced Kamala would be his number two, which wasn't much of a surprise given how few options he had left himself.

We've talked a lot about DEI on Fox in recent years and how anti-American it is if you're a believer in a merit-based system. DEI may officially stand for diversity, equity, and inclusion, but unofficially, at least in my book, it stands for . . .

Didn't.

Earn.

It.

Exhibit A is Kamala, who wasn't exactly chosen to be Biden's running mate because of her killer résumé on her LinkedIn page:

(Failed) District Attorney of San Francisco
(Failed) Attorney General of California
(Failed) Senator of California; rated most liberal of all in the Senate
(Failed) Presidential Candidate, 2019

But Biden's handlers weren't interested in her record or accomplishments. The only thought was checking off three boxes: Gender—check. Color—check. Attractive—check.

By declaring he would only choose a woman of color as his veep the same way he declared he would only appoint a female woman of color as a Supreme Court justice, Biden had boxed himself into a corner that left him three viable options as his running mate.

First was Susan Rice, (failed) national security adviser to Barack Obama. We all remember Rice, the senior official who said that Bowe Bergdahl, the Army sergeant who deserted his own unit and was later held captive by the Taliban, had served "with honor and distinction," which was a complete slap in the face to those he left behind. Rice eventually agreed to swap five Taliban prisoners for his release years later.

"He knowingly deserted and put thousands of people in danger because he did. We swore to an oath, and we upheld ours. He did not," Cody Full, a member of Bergdahl's platoon, said at the time. Honor and distinction don't seem to fit here.

Rice was also the national security savant who blamed a deadly attack on a U.S. consulate in Benghazi that left American ambassador Chris Stevens killed, along with U.S. Foreign Service information officer Sean Smith . . . on a spontaneous protest.

A bald-faced lie.

So given these stains on her résumé, and the fact she simply would have been a dud on the campaign trail, Rice was a nonstarter. Biden would be better off with Anne Rice, Jerry Rice, or Donna Rice than this Rice.

Second was Stacey Abrams, (twice failed) Georgia gubernatorial candidate and election denier. Yes, nothing says winner quite like Abrams, who was twice defeated by Brian Kemp in the Peach State despite getting the most favorable press coverage in the history of gubernatorial candidates. But she really had trouble accepting her defeat. Here are a few examples:

"It was not a free and fair election."

"There could not be free and fair elections in Georgia."

"No," I didn't lose—"I just didn't win."

"It was a stolen election. . . . They stole it from the voters of Georgia."

"I did win my election—I just didn't get to have the job."

The media never called out Abrams for this kind of rhetoric for whatever reason.

Abrams also had a slight ethics problem. Days before her second unsuccessful run against Kemp, *Politico* reported that "Abrams' campaign chair collected millions in legal fees from voting rights organization; Fair Fight Action, the nonprofit founded by Abrams, paid her close friend and ally's law firm $9.4 million in 2019 and 2020, with two more years of billing yet to be disclosed."

The lead paragraph: "The voting rights organization founded by Stacey Abrams spent more than $25 million over two years on legal fees, mostly on a single case, with the largest amount going to the self-described boutique law firm of the candidate's campaign chairwoman."

You get the idea. Abrams was the prequel to Fani Willis, the prosecutor in the (ridiculous) Trump legal case in Georgia that never saw the light of day thanks to Fani paying her (married) boyfriend more than

$600,000 of taxpayer money to try a RICO racketeering case despite never trying a RICO case in his life.

So that left Kamala as the only viable option for Biden to keep his pander promise. The Democratic ticket would go on to win the 2020 election by defying all laws of political physics by capturing more than 14 million more votes than Barack Obama did in 2008 despite running a basement campaign with a doddering old man and a cackling number two. Make of that what you will.

As vice president, Kamala was made the border czar to find the root causes of mass immigration. This in itself was a joke, considering that she once compared Immigration and Customs Enforcement (ICE) to the Ku Klux Klan, declared Trump's wall "medieval," and argued that illegal border crossings should be decriminalized. Putting her in charge of the border would be like hiring Bernie Madoff to be your financial wealth manager. And 12–15 million illegals coming into the country later, her performance was one of the biggest failures in American political history.

Kamala also signed off as the tiebreaking vote for the disastrous Inflation Reduction Act while also bragging about being "the last one in the room" on the deadly Afghanistan withdrawal that left thirteen U.S. military personnel dead.

Even her closest allies can't point to even one accomplishment she had as vice president.

So, with the hand to play with, the media had its biggest challenge ahead of them yet. After all, Barack was an easy sell because the guy was confident and knew how to give a speech. Hillary was unlikable, sure . . . but she could talk policy at length.

But Kamala? She was all frosting and no cake. Her brand would have to be remade from scratch, which meant doing an Etch A Sketch on virtually every radical position she held and attempting to sell to voters that, despite being vice president for the past three and a half years, she was actually the fresh, optimistic agent of change.

Right out of the gate, the coverage was positively surreal, exceeding even Pyongyang or Soviet levels. According to the Media Research Center, "MRC analysts reviewed all 100 campaign stories that aired on ABC's *World News Tonight* from the day Harris entered the race (July 21) through September 6, including weekends. Our analysts found 25 clearly positive statements about Harris from reporters, anchors, voters, or other non-partisan sources, with zero negative statements—none. That computes to a gravity-defying 100% positive spin score for the Vice President.

"As for Trump, our analysts found just five clearly positive comments, vs. 66 negative statements, for a dismal 7 percent positive (93% negative) spin score," it concludes.

Just incredible. Kamala goes 100-for-100 at the former home of journalistic heavyweights from David Brinkley to Barbara Walters to Frank Reynolds to Max Robinson to Ted Koppel despite her horrific record and major flip-flops.

New York magazine even took it a step further by putting a smiling Kamala sitting on top of a coconut with Democrats wildly cheering her below for a cover story I've since had framed.

"In a matter of days, Democrats discovered its future was actually in the White House all along," the July 29 cover reads.

Wow. So, only eight days after Biden was shivved aside, *New York* had vetted her enough: she was not only the future, she was the next *Evita*.

Throughout the rest of the summer, this is what the coverage in other outlets looked and sounded like:

NPR: Harris and Walz Reintroduce Joy to Democrats Their First Week on the Campaign Trail
Rolling Stone: Why Kamala Harris' New Politics of Joy Is the Best Way to Fight Fascism; History shows that joy and mockery are key to taking down existing or would-be authoritarian regimes
CNN: Kamala Harris Is tapping into the Black Joy Movement

Washington Post: Harris and Walz Seize on Positive
Message in Contrast to Darker Trump Themes

But what about Kamala's radical positions that helped sink her
2019 presidential campaign far earlier than expected? How will they
play out in the key Blue Wall states and border states like Arizona?

In regard to Pennsylvania, for example, Kamala was on record
saying she wants to ban all fracking. Here's what she said during a
CNN town hall in 2019:

> **Kamala:** *There's no question I'm in favor of banning fracking.
> And starting . . . with what we can do on day one around public
> lands, right? And then there has to be legislation, but yes—and
> this is something I've taken on in California. I have a history of
> working on this issue.*

> **Moderator Erin Burnett:** *So would you ban offshore drilling?*

> **Kamala:** *Yes, and I've again, worked on that. You can—you can
> talk to the folks in Santa Barbara about the work that I've done
> there where it's a big problem—but it's a big problem in many
> areas of our country—and yes, I would. Yes.*

> **Burnett:** *All right, two very definitive answers.*

They were definitive, weren't they? Zero ambiguity there. No more
fracking. No more offshore drilling. Period.

Fast-forward to September 2024 and Kamala's interview with
Dana Bash. Same network.

"As vice president, I did not ban fracking, and as president, I will not
ban fracking," Harris said.

This simply is not true. The Biden-Harris administration, within just
one week of taking office, signed an executive order called "Tackling the

Climate Crisis at Home and Abroad" that banned new oil and natural gas leasing on federal lands and waters.

What Kamala did here was classic lawyer BS, where yes, technically, *she* didn't ban new oil and natural gas leases (fracking) on federal lands and waters because it was *Biden* who signed the executive order.

Whatever. Harris knew she couldn't win Pennsylvania by being against fracking when it directly and indirectly employs hundreds of thousands of people in the state, so being the weathervane candidate she was, she said exactly what she had to say in an effort to get elected. Because without the Keystone State, her path would be next to impossible.

And that's just one example of many because she changed more positions than Simone Biles on an Olympic balance beam, including on:

- Banning plastic straws to save the environment
- Mandatory gun buyback programs as part of a gun safety initiative
- Reparations for slavery
- Building the wall (Team Kamala not only flipped on this, she even showed Trump's border wall in *her* campaign ads, insisting she would be tougher on the border)
- Banning private health insurance
- Using U.S. taxpayer money to pay for sex changes for illegals
- Medicare for All
- Protecting the filibuster

All of these positions were extreme, yes. But the last one regarding the filibuster is especially scary. If Kamala had won, she could have made good on her promise to eliminate the filibuster in the name of making abortion legal in all fifty states while usurping the Supreme Court in the process.

But you know it wouldn't end there: Democrats would ram through as many extreme changes to the fabric of the country as possible.

Puerto Rico and the District of Columbia would become U.S.

states, thereby giving the party four Democrat senators in perpetuity and likely a permanent majority in the Senate.

Dems would also undoubtedly expand the Supreme Court by four seats, resulting in a majority there as well.

Term limits would be slapped on Supreme Court justices.

The social media platform X would likely be regulated and censored or taken down altogether, all in the name of "protecting free speech from disinformation," like, you know . . . saying Covid came from a lab in Wuhan, China, that studies coronaviruses, or if arguing that fifty-one former intelligence officers like Leon Panetta and John Brennan were full of shit when they said the Hunter Biden laptop was a Russia plant to influence the election.

Voter ID would likely be banned nationally. As would the Electoral College.

And before you think Democrats would never go this far, I give you Senator Charles Ellis Schumer (D-NY). "We got it up to 48 [seats], but, of course, [Senator Krysten] Sinema and [Senator Joe] Manchin voted no; that's why we couldn't change the rules. Well, they're both gone," Schumer told reporters during the Democratic National Convention in August 2024, according to NBC News. Then–Arizona Democrat Senate candidate Ruben Gallego "is for it, and we have fifty-one. So, even losing Manchin, we still have fifty."

After the election, with Republicans easily taking back the Senate by a 53-47 margin, Chuck was singing a much different tune of bipartisanship.

"To my Republican colleagues, I offer a word of caution in good faith," Schumer said. "Take care not to misread the will of the people, and do not abandon the need for bipartisanship. After winning an election, the temptation may be to go to the extreme. We've seen that happen over the decades, and it has consistently backfired on the party in power.

"So, instead of going to the extremes, I remind my colleagues that this body is most effective when it's bipartisan. If we want the next four years in the Senate to be as productive as the last four, the only way that will happen is through bipartisan cooperation."

Oh, shut the front door, Chuck. You're just petrified that Republicans will do to you what you were openly plotting to do to them.

Anyway, the filibuster is alive and well for now. This perspective may not be popular, but here's hoping Republicans don't do what Schumer had planned if things went as he predicted. The filibuster exists for a very good reason: to provide checks and balances and compromise in a steady fashion instead of immediate power grabs that would result in massive upheaval and division in this country the likes we've never seen.

Dems will be back in power one day. That's just the way it works if history is any indication. And as Harry Reid beyond the grave and Mitch McConnell will tell you, all turnaround is fair play.

Going into post–Labor Day in September 2024, six weeks had passed since Biden exited stage left after having trouble finding the exit. Yet Kamala's people made sure she didn't do *one* interview during that stretch. Not with *The View*, not with Rachel Maddow, not one with sycophants like Colbert or Kimmel or Stern.

But in a post–Labor Day world when the joy of summer met the reality of autumn, Kamala's handlers finally decided to allow (hand-picked) media access in the lead-up to the first and only debate against Trump on September 10 on ABC. Of course they first turned to CNN, which agreed to do a pretaped interview to allow for editing before the final package aired.

The network also agreed to allow running mate Tim Walz to be by her side. The conversation with Bash looked like a parent-teacher conference, with the three sitting around an exceptionally small table in a poorly lit cafe in Savannah. Walz, who barely spoke and just stared at his potential future boss most of the time, towered over Kamala, who was hunched over for much of the interview and appeared nervous and unsteady despite the mostly friendly questions thrown her way.

Dana Bash: *Madam Vice President, Governor Walz, thank you so much for sitting down with me and bringing the bus. Bus tour is well underway here in Georgia. You have less time to make your case to voters than any candidate in modern American history. The voters are really eager to hear what your plans are. If you are elected, what would you do on day one in the White House?*

Harris: *Well, there are a number of things. I will tell you, first and foremost, one of my highest priorities is to do what we can to support and strengthen the middle class. When I look at the aspirations, the goals, the ambitions of the American people, I think that people are ready for a new way forward in a way that generations of Americans have been fueled by—by hope and by optimism.*

I think sadly in the last decade, we have had in the former president someone who has really been pushing an agenda and an environment that is about diminishing the character and the strength of who we are as Americans—really dividing our nation. And I think people are ready to turn the page on that.

Okay. Whatever that word salad was, it didn't answer the question about day one, so Bash *had* to follow up.

Bash: *So what would you do day one?*

Harris: *Day one, it's gonna be about one, implementing my plan for what I call an opportunity economy. I've already laid out a number of proposals in that regard, which include what we're gonna do to bring down the cost of everyday goods, what we're gonna do to invest in America's small businesses, what we're gonna do to invest in families.*

For example, extending the child tax credit to $6,000 for families for the first year of their child's life to help them buy a car seat, to help them buy baby clothes, a crib. There's the work

*that we're gonna do that is about investing in the American
family around affordable housing, a big issue in our country right
now. So there are a number of things on day one.*

Trump also offered a similar child tax credit, but okay. And Kamala
still didn't talk about how she was going to reduce prices on everyday
items like groceries and gas that she and Joe Biden were responsible for
in the first place.

At another point, Bash tried her very best to provide multiple-
choice answers for Harris to choose from in the question in an attempt
to avoid another situation where Kamala morphs into a human Chernobyl.

Bash: *Generally speaking, how should voters look at some of the
changes that you've made—that you explained some of here—
in your policy? Is it because you have more experience now and
you've learned more about the information? Is it because you're
running for president in a Democratic primary? And should they
feel comfortable and confident that what you're saying now is
gonna be your policy moving forward?*

Note: Bash would *never* be that gentle with any Republican in presenting so many get-out-of-jail-free cards in one question. But alas:

Harris: *Dana, I think the—the—the most important and most
significant aspect of my policy perspective and decisions is my
values have not changed. You mentioned the Green New Deal. I
have always believed, and I have worked on it, that the climate
crisis is real, that it is an urgent matter to which we should apply
metrics that include holding ourselves to deadlines around time.*

". . . holding ourselves to deadlines around time."
WTF? What other possible thing can deadlines be held against?
Hugh Hewitt had a similar thought at the time. "'Deadlines around

time.' As opposed to, say, deadlines around space?" the popular radio host mused.

"All Kamala had to get through was a pre-taped sit-down interview with reporters handpicked by her handlers while flanked by her emotional support VP and still managed to go on tangents about the significance of 'deadlines around time,'" observed Benny Johnson on X.

With that disaster out of the way, the biggest moment of Kamala's life was coming in just a few days. This was a make-or-break evening since so few Americans still didn't know who she was and what she stood for.

But as usual, she was going to need a major assist from the media, and especially from the moderators at ABC News.

She had a very big ace in the hole in the form of one of her oldest and dearest friends, near the top of ABC-owned Disney.

The Midwest Dad That Wasn't

Trump is going to lose. It will not be particularly close. He will receive fewer votes than in 2020, and Harris will receive even more votes than Biden did. Trump will lose more states than he did in 2020.

—JEFF TIMMER, LINCOLN PROJECT

Kamala Harris was riding high heading into August.

It was the perfect storm for such a flawed person and candidate. Where else but in the current Democratic Party could you run for president five years earlier, run a horrible campaign, drop out before even getting to Iowa, but still get chosen to be the nominee's running mate?

And then, after nearly four years of failure as vice president that was so bad that some in the press were openly asking if you should even *be* on the ticket again, your boss is thrown under the bus by members of your own party after they realized he couldn't win. He eventually gets shown the door just three and a half months before the election.

Your party still doesn't want you at the top of the ticket, but only you have access to a war chest with $350 million to spend, so they're stuck with choosing you to be the nominee.

Imagine this: Kamala Harris, who some former staffers say has an issue with doing *actual work*, is handed the nomination without having to earn one vote from the public. She avoids primary challengers, who surely would have beaten her the same way they did in 2019. She avoids multiple debates. And with such a short runway, her campaign won't be the usual twenty months or so, but about one hundred days.

With the convention coming up, Kamala had to make her first big choice. Who would she choose to be her vice president? Sitting out there was Pennsylvania governor Josh Shapiro, who enjoyed an approval rating in *the 60s* in the most crucial of battleground states. Shapiro gives good speeches, doesn't come across as radical but as a moderate, and could truly make a difference in winning those nineteen electoral votes.

This wasn't even a two-foot putt, it was a *two-inch* putt.

And, of course, she completely blew it for reasons that, to this day, make absolutely no sense.

"I am proud to announce that I've asked @Tim_Walz to be my running mate. As a governor, a coach, a teacher, and a veteran, he's delivered for working families like his. It's great to have him on the team. Now let's get to work. Join us," Kamala announced on X with a link to her donation page.

So why did she go this route? Maybe it was because Walz called JD Vance "weird" over and over in the weeks prior to the decision. This got cheers from the media—which was as harsh on Vance as they were on Trump—and the weird thing went viral for some reason on social media.

"These guys are creepy and yes, just weird as hell," Walz told reporters to chuckles from the objective press.

On cue, our unserious media threw up hot takes. An Associated Press headline: "How Tim Walz Became Beloved by Young Voters with a Message That the GOP Is 'Weird.'"

In this piece by what is supposed to be a neutral wire service, the AP turned to a historian at Texas A&M University who just so happened to write an anti-Trump book about his rhetoric. This is called shaping a narrative. A fixed fight.

"The opposite of normalizing authoritarianism is to make it weird, to call it out and to sort of mock it," Professor Jennifer Mercieca said. "To say, 'Hey, that's a weird thing you're doing, calling your opposition enemies instead of saying that they're good people who have different policy preferences.'"

Uh-huh. The thing is, people who use terms like *normalization* don't tend to understand what actual normal people find weird. As we'd all find out a few months later.

CBS News, which completely debased itself during the vice presidential debate, which we'll get to in a bit, also got in on the charade of portraying Walz as popular in Minnesota: "Walz, the popular two-term governor of Minnesota, could help Harris shore up support in Michigan, Wisconsin and Pennsylvania—Midwestern 'blue wall' states that have historically supported Democrats."

Popular, huh? Well, a poll taken before Walz was chosen showed that just 22 percent of Minnesotans felt he was a good choice to be Kamala's running mate. And after the ballots were counted on November 5, Harris-Walz took the state by only 4 points. In 2020, Biden-Harris defeated Trump by 7 points, showing he was a drag on the ticket in his home state. Trump also won Minnesota's First Congressional District, which was represented for thirteen years by . . . Tim Walz. He actually hurt her performance in his home state!

Buyer's remorse seemed to have set in pretty quick. What was it? The profoundly awkward and desperate way he practically begged a crowd for attention? The way he made Jeb Bush look like he had the machismo of Hulk Hogan? If Tim Walz was such a great pick, why did Kamala's team instruct the goofy eighties sitcom dad not to talk to the press after he was selected?

What? Yeah, that's what happened. For example, take what Walz did when a reporter asked him at the Minnesota State Fair on Labor Day weekend about the news that six hostages had been executed by Hamas in Gaza.

"What's your reaction to the six hostages being found in Gaza?" he was asked.

Walz, holding a milkshake, ignored the question and instead told the crowd, "Thanks, everybody!" before running off.

The video of Walz turning into Christian McCaffrey to escape a question quickly went viral, prompting the campaign to have him write the following on X.

"The anguish of losing a child is something no family should have to endure. Gwen and I send our deepest condolences to the Goldberg-Polin family, after Hamas' murder of their son Hersh," he apparently wrote. "Hamas is a brutal terrorist organization—and we condemn their continued atrocities against both Americans and Israelis in the strongest possible terms."

Okay, so why couldn't you say that at the fair, Governor?

Unless (gasp) Tim Walz is just as scripted as his running mate and has little ability to speak outside of scripted remarks too.

Walz's positions on basically everything, when combined with Kamala's, gave the United States its most radical, most extreme, most socialist ticket in this country's history. She could have moved to the center with Shapiro but craptastically chose to go as far to the left as possible with her soulmate Walz, who was basically AOC with a Midwest accent.

Again, this made zero sense. It also showed Kamala had some of the worst political instincts we've ever witnessed.

"I grew up in a small town," Walz said in his folksy announcement speech, echoing Kamala's "I grew up in a middle-class family" line.

"JD Vance is dead wrong about what makes small-town America tick," he continued. "Small towns don't work because everyone is closed-minded and prejudiced. They work because people mind their own damn business. JD Vance seems to have a real problem minding his."

Ummmm . . . okay.

Since when had JD Vance suggested prejudice made small towns tick? And since when had Tim Walz been a proponent of minding his own business? In a related story, Walz actually created a Covid snitch hotline at the height of the pandemic, encouraging neighbors to rat each other out for breaking his extreme protocols. The hotline endured through 2022. That's not exactly minding one's own business.

"When somebody tells who they are, they—believe them," Walz also said upon being chosen. "He [Trump] said he would ban abortion across this country, and he'll do it whether or not Congress is there or not."

That's just 100 percent false. Trump supports a ban at fifteen weeks and states' rights to individually decide on the issue, which correctly leaves decisions around abortion up to the voters, not up to executive decisions at the federal level.

"Like all regular people I grew up with in the heartland, JD studied at Yale," Walz said to laughter at a rally in Philadelphia in August. "He had his career funded by Silicon Valley billionaires, and then wrote a bestseller trashing that community."

So, working your way out of a broken home and poverty, joining the Marines out of high school, and graduating from Yale is somehow a bad thing?

Walz also presented himself as Mr. Ordinary, with totally ordinary and moderate opinions. But do these sound like moderate positions?

Walz supports sex changes for minors without parental permission.

He's for open borders and illegal crossings—and even told CNN in 2019 that he wanted to invest in a "ladder company" to help illegal migrants get over Trump's border wall.

He supports sanctuary cities.

He supports a carbon-free electrical grid by 2040 in Minnesota, which has some of the coldest weather in the country.

He installed tampon machines in *boys' elementary school bathrooms*.

He supports free health care and free college for illegal immigrants, and giving them driver's licenses to boot.

He supported a mandatory mask mandate in Minnesota.

And, of course, he presided over the state during its 2020 riots, which resulted in $500 million in damage in Minneapolis, including the torching of a police precinct. Walz refused for days to quell the violence by bringing in the National Guard. And when he finally did, he actually *apologized* to rioters when he pulled the trigger after it was far too late.

But this is where Walz really crossed the line, at least with me.

Someone thought it was a great idea to have Walz and AOC play each other in a football videogame (*Madden*) on Twitch. The campaign had continually pushed Walz as the high school football version of Vince Lombardi, so they figured this would underscore his bona fides with the voters they needed in Big Ten country.

"In Minnesota, we trust a coach who turned a team that was 0-27 into state champions!" Senator Amy Klobuchar (D-MN) exclaimed in her speech during the Democratic National Convention.

But before we get to the punch line, it is fair to ask: Was Walz a head coach at the high school that turned a 0-27 team into state champions back in the 1990s?

Nope. He was an assistant *volunteer* coach.

And *why* was he only a volunteer coach, one might also ask?

Because this maniac decided it was a good idea to drink his face off, get into his car, and drive (checks notes) 96 miles per hour. He got pulled over and was charged with DUI after registering a 0.128 blood alcohol level, well above the legal limit.

Walz actually got lucky. He could have killed someone driving like that while intoxicated. And it's not like he did this as a foolish teenager: He was in his thirties at the time. He was a teacher. Great example, Gov.

So, with that DUI on his record, Walz couldn't be hired. He could only be a part of the coaching staff as a volunteer.

The thing is, Walz has always been a prolific liar. He even tried to say he wasn't charged with DUI, which is one of the easiest things to fact-check.

Per a CNN report:

A CNN KFile review of statements made by the Walz campaign at the time reveals numerous discrepancies between how the campaign described the events and the facts of what actually took place that night.

"The DUI charge was dropped for a Reason: it wasn't true," Walz's then-campaign communications director told local news in 2006. "The trooper had him drive to the station and then leave on his own after being at the station. Tim feels bad about speeding and has paid the ticket and apologized to his family at the time it happened."

But, according to CNN, that's not what happened. At all.

"In fact, the incident's police report clearly states that Walz was transported by police to a local hospital for blood alcohol testing after being arrested. And this week, Nebraska state police confirmed to CNN that Walz was taken by a state trooper to jail."

Okay then . . .

Back to the *Madden* game against AOC: Walz decided to share how things were going on social media.

"@AOC can run a mean pick 6 - and I can call an audible on a play. And we both know that if you take the time to draw up a playbook, you're gonna use it," Walz tweeted.

Run a mean pick-6? How do you "run" a pick-6, exactly?

For those readers who are not too savvy about football (and Walz himself is clearly in that category), let me explain: A pick-6 is an interception by the defense that gets returned for a touchdown. It's spontaneous. It just . . . happens sometimes. Maybe a throw is tipped at the line. Maybe the defender jumps the route at the perfect, precise moment. You don't "run" anything. It's not a play. You can't draw it up in a playbook. No person who has coached football, played it, or watched it has ever spoken like this.

After major blowback, "Coach" deleted the tweet. And this campaign wonders how it didn't attract more male voters.

But even worse than the DUI, the lie after the DUI, or scheming to create pick-6s was Walz's tales around his National Guard service and using "weapons of war" on the battlefield. The thing is, "Coach" never saw a battlefield after he abandoned his unit after learning they were being deployed to Iraq during the war.

"If you sold out your Guard unit and abandoned them, what are you going to do at the national level?" one veteran asked in reference to the possibility of Walz becoming vice president during an interview on Megyn Kelly's podcast.

"I call him a coward because he is," a second veteran told Megyn, while a third called him a "military impersonator" after it was revealed Walz lied repeatedly about his rank.

"What bothers me about Tim Walz is this stolen valor garbage. Do not pretend to be something that you're not," JD Vance, a former Marine, said at a campaign event in Michigan. "I'd be ashamed if I was him, and I lied about my military service like he did."

"In making the case for why weapons of war should never be on our streets or in our classrooms, the governor misspoke," a campaign spokesperson said in attempting to clean up aisle 5. "He did handle weapons of war and believes strongly that only military members trained to carry those deadly weapons should have access to them, unlike Donald Trump and JD Vance, who prioritize the gun lobby over our children."

Oh, good grief. You're going to turn this into a "Will anyone think of the children?!" moment? And no, you don't misspeak about being in war zones, just like you don't misspeak about where you were in moments like the Tiananmen Square Massacre in 1989.

But he did it again, this time claiming to be in Hong Kong when the horrific event was unfolding.

"As a young man, I was just going to teach high school in Foshan in Guangdong, and was in Hong Kong in May of '89. As the events were unfolding, several of us went in," Walz said during a 2014 hearing marking the massacre's twenty-fifth anniversary. "I still remember the train station in Hong Kong."

Wow. Lots of detail there. It's like it just happened yesterday.

Like Biden, Walz enjoyed bragging about being there when the deadly human rights crackdown went down.

"I was in Hong Kong on June 4, 1989, when, of course, Tiananmen

Square happened. And I was in China after that. It was very strange 'cause, of course, all outside transmissions were, were blocked—Voice of America—and, of course, there was no, no phones or email or anything. So I was kind of out of touch. It took me a month to know the Berlin Wall had fallen when I was living there," he also said in 2019.

One problem: Walz was twelve thousand miles away from Hong Kong and was back in Nebraska at the time, according to Minnesota Public Radio News and the *Washington Free Beacon*, who both actually did some digging and actual journalism.

Overall, Walz has said he visited China thirty times. What was his fascination with this communist country? Who goes to any foreign country thirty times, especially that one?

Back to the weird argument that got Kamala's attention when it came to Walz. Get this.

Before they got married, Tim's wife, Gwen Walz, told a Nebraska newspaper that the couple wanted to get married on the exact date (June 4) of the Tiananmen Square Massacre because "he wanted to have a date he'll always remember."

And sure enough, on June 4, 1994, the five-year anniversary of the massacre, Tim and Gwen Walz happily got hitched. That's beyond weird.

Then again, this is the same Gwen Walz who said this during the Minneapolis riots in 2020: "I could smell the burning tires, and that was a very real thing." She added this doozy: "I kept the windows open as long as I could because I felt like that was such a touchstone of what was happening."

Innocent people died. Businesses were destroyed. A police station was burned to the ground. And this freak said she wanted to smell the destruction because it was a "touchstone of what was happening"?

Joe Rogan had heard enough from the Walzes, and later revealed after the election that he jumped in to endorse Trump primarily because of Tim Walz.

"You're telling me that you don't care if someone is a liar? You don't care if they lie about their military rank, where they served?" Rogan asked rhetorically on his podcast in December 2024. "You don't care if they lie about being as assistant [coach]? You don't care if they lie about Tiananmen Square? There are just too many things. This is so crazy. You would get fired if you were an assistant manager at a fucking oil-change company."

These weren't your daddy's Democrats anymore, that's for certain. *Radical* may be too forgiving a word to apply to the current iteration of the donkey's party.

Substance was becoming a problem for Kamala Harris after voters began expressing concerns that she didn't have any when it came to her plans for the country if elected. In fact, her campaign began to resemble the most popular sitcom of all time. And that wasn't a good thing.

Kamala Seinfeld:
A Campaign About Nothing

I think [the debate] will cost him, yes. I'm trying to decide if I wanna go on record, and the answer's yes. I think that [Trump] loses because of this debate performance.

—FRANK LUNTZ, GOP POLLSTER

Philadelphia. The home to the best fictional fights of all time . . . namely *Rocky I* and *Rocky II.* A nonfictional fight, that of the rhetorical variety, was also set to take place in the City of Brotherly Love (the person who came up with that slogan clearly has never been to a Cowboys-Eagles game). Donald Trump versus Kamala Harris.

For Trump, this debate marked his chance to put away his challenger nearly two months before Election Day. Kamala was like a boxer who decided to avoid all training and sparring before getting into a heavyweight bout. Trump had already vanquished Biden in June in more ways than one: he not only won that debate, but he also effectively made Biden a one-term president.

The debate was moderated by ABC, which had already signaled that this wasn't even the network of Peter Jennings anymore by the way it went about its journalistic business since Kamala was installed as the Democratic nominee, providing (as mentioned in the book previously) her with one hundred positive stories and zero negative ones.

Even Baghdad Bob would say after seeing a stat like that, "Hey, guys, aren't you laying it on a bit thick there?"

So ABC was an extension of Kamala's PR team. Check. The question was why were they being so overt about it? For the answer, follow the ladder to the top of ABC News.

Her name is Dana Walden. She's the same age as Kamala Harris. She was California-born, just like Kamala. In fact, they're just ten days apart in age. Walden lives in a really nice neighborhood, just as Kamala does again now with her husband, Doug Emhoff, in the ritzy Brentwood section of Los Angeles, once the home of O. J. Simpson.

Wait? Do these two know each other? Well, as a matter of fact, not only are they acquaintances, but they are seemingly besties, having known each other since 1994. Dana even set up Kamala with Emhoff on a blind date years back.

"In many ways, Dana and Matt are responsible for my marriage," Kamala cackled at a fundraiser at the Waldens' home in Brentwood in 2022.

Matt Walden, Dana's husband, and Emhoff have been close friends since the 1980s, according to the *New York Times*.

"The Waldens—'extraordinary friends,' per the vice president— have donated money to Ms. Harris's political campaigns since at least 2003, when she ran for district attorney in San Francisco."

So why do we care about any of this stuff? Well, you'll never guess who runs ABC News.

Dana Walden.

So maybe, I don't know . . . there was a *slight* conflict of interest going into this ABC News debate, given Kamala Harris's closest friend was potentially calling the shots on what questions would be asked, who would and would not be fact-checked and subject to follow-up questions, and who might get the questions in advance.

Now, before you say that no news organization would *ever* provide a candidate questions in advance to help them win a presidential contest, look no further than CNN in 2016. On two occasions the network provided Hillary Clinton's camp with questions in advance of town halls it was hosting.

It was all laid out in the WikiLeaks email dumps, and there was zero ambiguity around it happening. It did, as CNN later admitted as such, before firing Donna Brazile for being partly responsible along with former CNN blowhard Roland Martin. Despite this ethical breach and taking advantage of the access CNN allowed in terms of getting her hands on some of the questions, Brazile still can be seen on most Sundays providing political analysis while lecturing audiences on the ethical shortcomings of Donald Trump.

The entity that currently employs Brazile? Dana Walden's ABC News.

So, from the start of this rhetorical bout that was more like a WWE match in that it was decided well in advance, it was obvious Trump was in a three-on-one situation, with Trump not only battling lightweight Kamala Harris, but also the moderators David Muir and Linsey Davis, who overall asked only one question of the economy, no questions on crime, one question on the border, no questions on education, no questions on the Afghanistan withdrawal, no questions on China, no questions on Ukraine, no questions on the Middle East. But the duo *was* able to find time for questions on January 6 and abortion and climate change and the wonders of Obamacare, because ABC's goal was to avoid as much as possible Kamala's vice presidential record on the issues that matter most.

Despite all the advantages, Kamala still had to make the sale, especially on the economy and bringing down the cost of items Americans buy on a regular basis. And she absolutely blew it. Please do me a favor. Read this first answer out loud to yourself or to someone near you, then tell me if there's even one takeaway here that makes you believe this person has a clue how to lower inflation or run the U.S. economy in general.

Muir: *When it comes to the economy, do you believe Americans are better off than they were four years ago?*

Harris: *So, I was raised as a middle-class kid. And I am actually the only person on this stage who has a plan that is about lifting*

*up the middle class and working people of America. I believe in
the ambition, the aspirations, the dreams of the American people.
And that is why I imagine and have actually a plan to build
what I call an opportunity economy. Because here's the thing. We
know that we have a shortage of homes and housing, and the cost
of housing is too expensive for far too many people. We know that
young families need support to raise their children. And I intend
on extending a tax cut for those families of $6,000, which is the
largest child tax credit that we have given in a long time. So that
those young families can afford to buy a crib, buy a car seat, buy
clothes for their children.*

*My passion, one of them, is small businesses. I was actually—
my mother raised my sister and me, but there was a woman who
helped raise us. We call her our second mother. She was a small
business owner. I love our small businesses. My plan is to give a
$50,000 tax deduction to startup small businesses, knowing they
are part of the backbone of America's economy.*

So much to unpack here—if you can even make it through that word salad of platitudes.

For starters, you gotta love Kamala saying she's the only one who has a plan "about lifting the middle class and working people of America." If she had a plan, why the hell hadn't it been implemented *already*?

Next, this was an answer that was absolutely rehearsed, as if she knew this exact question was coming. Why else would she go into stump-speech mode with the bullshit about being a middle-class kid and believing the ambition, aspirations, and the dreams of the American people? It's beyond phony and inauthentic.

This is the *Seinfeld* candidate: a campaign about nothing.

And no, joy and vibes ain't a strategy or policy. In the end, it's still the Biden clown car with a different coat of paint.

Finally, how again does extending a tax cut of $6,000 bring down the cost of groceries, or rent, or gas? This too is BS because Kamala was also going to let the Trump tax cuts expire, which would have wiped out (and then some) the $6,000 tax cut for families. And if you're in a single-person household, as more younger people are than ever before, this tax cut wouldn't apply to you.

As for the $50,000 tax deduction for small businesses, she never gets around to how that would be paid for, especially under a scenario, which came to fruition, where Republicans controlled the House and Senate.

In other words, this canned answer was an epic failure. And the amazing thing is, her handlers had her repeat it over and over at rallies and in interviews moving forward. Talk about tone-deaf.

Donald Trump was not at his best that night since he was constantly battling three opponents, not one, but his closing argument was strong and pointed. "She just started by saying she's going to do this, she's going to do that. She's going to do all these wonderful things," Trump correctly stated. "Why hasn't she done it? She's been there for three and a half years."

That's exactly right.

Predictably, the moderators didn't make illegal immigration, the number two issue in the country (per Gallup and other polls), the subject of their next question. Rather, they talked about (ding! ding! ding!) abortion. This was when Linsey Davis conducted the first of five fact-checks of Trump without fact-checking Kamala once despite having multiple opportunities to do so.

Here's one example of Davis fact-checking Trump on the issue of late-term abortion and even post-birth abortion, only to get the fact-check wrong.

"They have abortion in the ninth month. They even have, and you can look at the governor of West Virginia [Virginia], the previous governor . . . not the current governor, who is doing an excellent job, but the governor before, he said, 'The baby will be born, and we will decide what to do with the baby,' in other words we'll execute the baby," Trump said.

Davis was ready for this answer, as Trump had been noting comments made by then–Virginia governor Ralph Northam for years. Northam said at the time: "The infant would be delivered. The infant would be kept comfortable. The infant would be resuscitated if that's what the mother and the family desired."

And if the mother and family didn't want the infant resuscitated? Well, you know what happens next.

No matter. Davis went right through that red light to have her moment.

"There is no state in this country where it is legal to kill a baby after it's born," Davis declared before quickly moving on.

And here's the thing: *the fact-check itself is wrong.* Take Tim Walz's Minnesota, for example. According to the Minnesota Department of Health, in 2021 during his first term as governor, five babies were born after incomplete abortions and subsequently died. In 2019, three babies born after incomplete (botched) abortions in the state died. Overall, according to the U.S. Centers for Disease Control and Prevention, "between 2003 and 2014, around 143 babies died after being born alive following failed abortions."

"It's a fact that, as a U.S. senator, Kamala Harris voted against protections for babies born alive after failed abortions. And as a member of Congress, her running mate Tim Walz even issued a public apology for 'accidentally' voting for said legislation after he previously voted against it," wrote Susan B. Anthony Pro-Life America president Marjorie Dannenfelser in a letter to ABC News. Dannenfelser also asked for a meeting with ABC while also requesting Davis correct the record. Both requests, of course, were ignored.

Through the rest of the evening, Trump was fact-checked another four times, while being asked six follow-up questions. Kamala received zero fact-checks, as noted earlier, and was not asked even one follow-up.

And again, these alleged fact-checks were wrong. Excuse me for getting emotional on this topic, but I think I speak for anyone clamoring for objective, truthful journalism and not whatever slop Dana Walden's ABC News served up that night.

"Crime here is up and through the roof despite their fraudulent statements that they made," Trump said at another point in the evening. "Crime in this country is through the roof."

"President Trump, as you know, the FBI says overall violent crime is actually coming down in this country," David Muir piously responded.

The FBI (after the debate, of course) backed Trump's assertion up when the agency magically put out a revision to its crime stats.

"After reporting there was a 2.1% drop in violent crimes in 2022, the FBI now admits there was actually a 4.5% increase," Fox News reported. "According to crime and data expert John Lott, the new numbers reflect a net increase of 80,029 violent crimes in 2022 over 2021. He found that under the umbrella of violent crime, there were an additional 1,699 murders, 7,780 rapes, 33,459 robberies and 37,091 aggravated assaults that year."

Yep. More than 80,000 violent crimes over the span of one year under Biden-Harris definitely qualifies as "through the roof." Trump was also correct in also noting that the original FBI report didn't include cities with the highest crime rates in the country. FBI director Christopher Wray couldn't have been gone fast enough.

Muir has yet to correct the record on *World News Tonight* and ABC wouldn't respond to Fox's request for comment. Go figure.

Trump rightly took to Truth Social to slam Muir on September 26.

Now you don't know this, but we had a deal with ABC that there will be no corrections of any kind, and they violated the deal. Why? Because they're bad people, and they're fake news. So he did it many times to me during the debate. He violated the deal. That's the deal, because you can take anything and try and make up stories with it. We had a deal where that wouldn't happen. You could do whatever you wanted as soon as the debate was over, but he did it in total violation of what our agreement was. And a lot of people standing right over there [as he looked toward his staff] will tell you exactly what it was, will show you what it was. David Muir has lost all credibility.

At another point, Trump correctly reminded voters that Kamala is for taxpayer-funded sex changes for illegals in prison.

"She wants to do transgender operations on illegal aliens that are in prison. This is a radical left liberal that would do this," he noted.

This is where the fact-checkers chimed in on social media and on other networks.

"What the hell was he talking about? No one knows, which was, of course, exactly Harris's point," the insufferable Susan Glasser of *New York* magazine huffed on X, while Wolf Blitzer called Trump's claim "outlandish."

It's not just bias. It's just plain lazy, especially in a world where a simple Google search can verify Trump's claim in under ten seconds that Kamala herself said she pushed to provide "gender transition surgery for state inmates." She also signed a petition in 2019 that called for taxpayers to pay for sex changes for inmates who are here illegally.

The *New York Times* eventually conceded that the "wildest sounding attack line" from Trump was "basically true." However, the final conclusion of the fact-check was not "True" or even "Mostly True" but "This needs context."

What absolute hacks these people are.

So while Trump was spitting facts, Kamala was allergic to them throughout the ninety-minute debate.

ABC had by my count more than a dozen opportunities to fact-check Kamala Harris—and the moderators refused to do so.

Here are some examples of lies Harris told at the debate without any pushback from Muir and Davis.

Harris said that under the Biden-Harris administration, there are no military personnel in active war zones. Yet Muir and Davis said nothing. They *had* to know we have 900 U.S. military personnel in

Syria, with another 2,500 U.S. troops in Iraq. We've seen personnel being attacked and killed in the Red Sea this year from drone strikes by Iranian-backed proxies.

Crickets.

Kamala also claimed Trump supports a national ban on abortion (lie) and in vitro fertilization, or IVF (lie). On the latter, Trump said he supports the government helping couples in need to pay for it, while he has repeatedly stressed that he agrees with the Supreme Court sending the issue back to the states (and therefore the public) on the former.

She insisted that she's been pro-fracking for years. It's an odd claim considering Biden-Harris banned public fracking in the first week of the administration and she didn't make one public comment on the issue as vice president, or at least until she needed to win Pennsylvania as the nominee.

Kamala also claimed that night that "Donald Trump left us the worst unemployment since the Great Depression."

This claim was not even remotely close to being true and there is crucial context to add here: The unemployment rate was 6.4 percent at the end of Trump's term, but that was overwhelmingly due to the pandemic. Prepandemic, in February 2020 (everything shut down in mid-March, you may recall), the unemployment rate was at a historic low, just 3.5 percent.

By the way, unemployment was 7.9 percent after four years of Barack Obama and 7.2 percent after eight years of George W. Bush. It jumped to 10 percent in October 2009. So, no, Biden-Harris weren't handed the worst unemployment since the Great Depression. This was so easy to fact-check, but that wasn't the assignment Muir and Davis were given.

I can go on with the list of lies but there's so much fun to get to in this book.

A note on the "they're eating the dogs" in Springfield, Ohio, line. I'm sure Trump wanted that one back with so many other verifiable examples to choose from regarding the damage to quality of life and safety in this country. The spin afterward from the media was hysterical in focusing on that one sentence from Trump, but it wasn't remotely damaging.

I was invited to join Bill Hemmer and Dana Perino on *America's Newsroom* the following day for postdebate analysis. If you're at work and can't catch the show live, do make a point to record it. Sitting with the two anchors and watching them prepare for each segment like the journalism version of Navy SEALs is a pleasure to watch. If the broadcast appears as smooth as it looks and sounds at home, do know there's a very good reason why. And you won't meet two more real and agreeable people in the business. After the debate, the chattering class all agreed that Kamala was the big winner. No doubt. Anyone who said otherwise was delusional.

As I wrote in the *New York Post* the following day, oftentimes there's a decided night-and-day gap between what the media perceives as public perception and *actual* public perception when it comes to Donald Trump. Just think back to the 2016 campaign as a prime example when the Blue Wall and Trump's chances there was completely ignored.

Same goes for this debate between Trump and Harris.

Compare these headlines.

"Harris Dominates as Trump Gets Defensive: 6 Takeaways from the Debate" was the lead headline in the *New York Times*.

"Harris Dominated Trump in Debate, but Will It Matter?" was the *Washington Post*'s take.

But after the debate and after many in the media swooned over their new queen in Harris, a funny thing happened: polls and focus groups emerged showing her winning on style points but Trump winning on substance.

Take this Reuters focus group: Ten undecided voters were asked how they would vote after watching the debate. Six said they would now vote for Trump, while just three said they'd vote for Harris. One was undecided.

Over at C-SPAN, its online poll also shows a decided Trump victory, with Trump receiving close to *three-quarters* of the vote when asking who won.

Meanwhile, CNN's postdebate poll showed Trump expanding a commanding lead when it comes to which candidate can handle the economy best. Before the debate, Trump's lead was 18 points on this number one issue; after the debate it had grown to a 20-point margin.

So why the disconnect?

Here's one theory: Kamala was too rehearsed. Her answers were too canned. And on substance, the public still had no idea how she was going to lower the cost of living.

We still had no idea how she would lower violent crime that is causing exoduses out of dozens of cities, including New York, Chicago, Minneapolis, and San Francisco.

On the border, most sane and sober people did not believe she could fix the border she helped open, a move that led to the mass illegal immigration that is crippling city budgets and exhausting social services.

What was her plan for wars overseas? What was her trade and tariff position with China? Was she still all in on government price-fixing? Did she still really think taxing unrealized capital gains was a good idea? Did she think men can get pregnant? Did she still want American taxpayers to pay for sex changes for illegals?

That's why I told Bill and Martha the next morning that the onus was on Kamala to make the sale, not Trump, despite him getting all of the focus that day. We knew what we were getting with Trump on all of the aforementioned issues because *he was already president and has a record.* With Kamala, we also had a record as vice president, which is horrific, but we also had her contradicting her own positions, which were on tape for everyone to see.

Her worldview and plans for the country were as clear as mud before the debate, and they were the same way after it. Therefore, she didn't win, which may be why polls barely moved post-debate.

Also, one more thing no one talked about: If the Coconut Queen had such a great night in Philadelphia, why was she (*again*) prevented from doing interviews for days after the debate? If she had such command, why not build off that momentum?

Rhetorical questions.

Kamala went back on the campaign trail a few days later for stops in Pennsylvania and Michigan. Winning without sweeping the Blue Wall looked to be extremely difficult and polls showed she was struggling to win over male working-class voters.

Turns out the problem was far worse than the campaign realized, especially with one very key voting block Dems could *always* rely on.

Kamala's sizzle may have wowed the media, but it was Trump's steak—and his existing record as president—that ultimately mattered come November 5.

The "Positive" Side
Sends Another Assassin

If you're a last-minute voter, who is undecided, what have you seen that makes you want to vote for Donald Trump? And what have you seen that makes you want to vote for Kamala Harris? You've seen positive on one side . . . [while Trump's side] really hurts and demoralizes people.

—HILL HARPER, ACTOR, FAILED SENATE CANDIDATE

When I cohost *The Big Weekend Show*, it's not on a week-by-week basis. I'm part of a rotation with other contributors like Guy Benson, Nicole Saphier, Anita Vogel, Kennedy, Charlie Hurt, David Webb, Gianno Caldwell, Alicia Acuna, Lisa Boothe, Joey Jones, Tomi Lahren, Tammy Bruce, Jason Chaffetz, Katie Pavlich, and Tom Shillue, just to reel off a few names off the top of my head.

So on September 15, 2024, it marked just my second time hosting the show since the July 13 attempt on Trump in Butler. But as I was getting ready to go in, my phone began blowing up.

"They tried to kill him again," one friend wrote.

"These motherfuckers aren't going to stop until Trump's dead," said another.

I immediately turned to Fox to see what the hell was going on after reading no shots were actually fired at Trump. And I remember thinking that the network wasn't scheduled to carry any Trump rallies that day, nor was there anything in the early show rundown. So where could this attempt have happened?

As you know, the ambush was to occur at Trump International Golf Course in West Palm Beach, Florida, just a few miles from Trump's Mar-a-Lago resort. Trump didn't have the round on his schedule but was known to play on the rare days he wasn't campaigning.

Reports began to come in that the gunman had been identified as Ryan Routh, a wackjob so obsessed with the Russia-Ukraine war that he went to Kyiv to volunteer to join the Ukrainian army. Even they rejected Routh, calling him "not the ideal candidate."

For the assassination attempt, Routh, fifty-eight, camped out for twelve hours outside the sixth hole and created and hid in a sniper's nest in some bushes near a fence not far from the green. Fortunately a Secret Service agent noticed the barrel of a rifle sticking out through the fence as Trump was finishing up on the fifth hole. The agent fired at him but missed, and Routh fled by car. He was later stopped and arrested without resisting.

If Routh hadn't been discovered, it is almost certain Trump would be dead today. The gunman likely would have had a wide-open place to start shooting as Trump approached the green on the sixth hole with nothing to provide the former president for cover. It's horrifying to think about.

We ended up not preempting the show that evening and even extended it to two hours. We interviewed all sorts of former law enforcement members, former Secret Service and FBI agents, various lawmakers, and hosts like Sean Hannity and Mark Levin.

The show was one of the most-watched *Big Weekend Show* episodes ever, but it was the kudos we received from viewers and producers alike that really made you appreciate being able to deliver in big situations like that. For me, despite not being a regular host on the network, it felt completely natural.

But like the first assassination attempt in Pennsylvania, attempt number two warranted many questions. For starters, how did Routh know that Trump would be golfing there that day? Again, it was never announced. Trump also plays at another Trump course not far from Mar-a-Lago, in Jupiter, Florida. But perhaps Routh just made a guess, and if it was wrong, he would just try again another weekend.

But here was the bigger question: How was a gunman able to set up a sniper's nest and remain there for twelve *hours* without any Secret Service agents discovering him? Surely agents were doing a sweep in and around the course before Trump arrived to ensure a secure perimeter, right?

Right?

Nope. That never happened. And this was just sixty-three days after Trump was *shot*. You'd think the Secret Service would know they had dodged a bullet—for lack of a better term—in Butler because Trump miraculously turned his head hard to the right at the exact right time. Now maybe they would double their efforts to secure all possible locations where a would-be assassin would have line of sight to Trump.

But that didn't happen here either. And don't tell me the Secret Service doesn't have the resources. The agency received more than $1 billion in 2024. In 2020, it was $754 million.

And by the way, not one person was fired after this attempt either. Why is that?

The Democrats' reckless rhetoric, echoed by the media, was shown to have inspired Routh. In a post on X in April, he wrote, "DEMOCRACY is on the ballot and we cannot lose. We cannot afford to fail. The world is counting on us to show the way."

Does "Democracy is on the ballot" sound familiar to you?

Here are some other examples of Democrats and even Biden himself all but begging crazy people to take out Trump.

"Trump is a threat to our democracy and fundamental freedoms," said Kamala Harris. But her running mate really took the cake with this reckless rhetoric.

Tim Walz warned, "Don't give them the power. Look—are they a threat to democracy? Yes. Are they going to take our rights away? Yes. Are they going to put people's lives in danger? Yes. Are they going to endanger the planet by not dealing with climate change? Yes. Everybody in this room knows—I know it, as a teacher: A bully has no self-confidence. A bully has no strength. They have nothing. The fascists depend on fear. The fascists depend on us going back, but we're not afraid of weird people."

That was Walz just *two weeks* after the first assassination attempt. What an assclown. Seriously.

"It is just unquestionable at this point that man cannot see public office again. He is not only unfit, he is destructive to our democracy, *and he has to be eliminated*," demanded Representative Dan Goldman (D-NY).

"The rhetoric you hear from the Republican Party is shameful and disgraceful for Latinos. And you know, when you see 'Latinos for Trump,' to me it is like seeing 'Jews for Hitler,' almost, you know?" That was Representative Vincente Gonzalez (D-TX).

And we couldn't leave Hillary out of this one, now could we?

"Hitler was duly elected, right? Trump is telling us what he intends to do. Take him at his word. The man means to throw people in jail who disagree with him, shut down legitimate press outlets, do what he can to literally undermine the rule of law and our country's values," opined Hillary on *The View*.

"Donald Trump is a threat to democracy, and saying so is not incitement. Opposing political violence does not mean ignoring authoritarianism," wrote the abhorrent Jonathan Chait (D–*New York* magazine) *one day* after the second assassination attempt.

There are other examples, but we've got finite space here. A poll from Gallup says it all: a whopping 83 percent of Americans say the media bears "a great deal" (47 percent) or "a moderate amount" (36 percent) of blame for political division in this country. Instead of informing us, it seeks to divide through fear and loathing.

It hasn't always been this way. In 1976, nearly three-quarters (72 percent) of the country had trust in the media. Even just twenty years ago, that number was an even 50-50 split.

In another poll released in October 2024, Gallup also reports that "the news media was also the least trusted group among 10 U.S. civic and political institutions involved in the democratic process, with surveyors trusting local governments the most.

"Americans' trust in the news media is at a new, record low, with only 31% expressing a 'great deal' or 'fair amount' of trust and confidence in the media to report the news 'fully, accurately and fairly,'" the report notes.

There's no going back from this.

Following the second attempt, many in the press, instead of asking how two gunmen could have both come so close to ending Trump's life, they simply let their default setting kick in.

Blame Trump.

Enter MSNBC on the day of the attempt in West Palm Beach after it was reported.

"Do you expect to hear anything from the Trump campaign about toning down the rhetoric, toning down the violence, or would that be atypical of the former president?" anchor Alex Witt asked guest Elise Jordan.

You read that correctly. It was *Trump*—the guy they called a Nazi-fascist-Hitler—who needed to adjust *his* rhetoric to avoid getting shot.

Okay, okay . . . that's MSNBC, Conch. We expect that from the loony bin.

Then Lester Holt from the mother ship says, "Hold my beer."

"Today's apparent assassination attempt comes amid increasingly fierce rhetoric on the campaign trail. Mr. Trump, his running mate JD Vance continue to make baseless claims about Haitian migrants," he said on *NBC Nightly News*.

Again, you don't hate the media enough. You think you do, but you don't.

Trump didn't play golf for the final seven weeks of the campaign, one of the things he loves to do most. Can you really blame him?

As we got closer to the election, it was time for the usual suspects to start handing out their endorsements, which was as predictable as the New York Jets not making the playoffs. But for Kamala, the slam-dunk endorsements were proving hard to come by. And for good reason.

The Endorsement Kamala Lacked: Forget *WaPo*, It Was the Teamsters That Mattered

The math has shown Donald Trump has no chance of winning in November of '24. He won't even win Georgia. If you're a Republican that can't win Georgia in November of '24, you have no shot.
—CHRIS SUNUNU, WHO LATER ENDORSED TRUMP

If there's one thing the Dems could always count on heading into any presidential election, it's endorsements.

Lots and lots of endorsements . . .

Let's start with newspapers, shall we? It's a stat you may have heard me share on Fox News. But for those who haven't, when I was at the *Hill*, we compiled a list of newspaper endorsements across the country, targeting the top 59 publications based on subscriptions in various locations. And out of those 59, Hillary Clinton received 57 endorsements to Donald Trump's 2.

So after Trump won quite easily in the Electoral College, it proved that media influence even eight years ago wasn't remotely what it once was. In fact, in 2024, it's almost nonexistent, given that the result this time around included Trump winning the popular vote.

But those who work in the industry really believe they still have enough influence to make a difference and get their candidates of choice elected. Just take a look at what happened over at the *Washington Post*, a newspaper that has *never* endorsed a Republican presidential candidate in its history, when it announced just a few days before the election it would not endorse Harris or Trump for president this time around.

Yup, the same publication that endorsed Jimmy Carter and Walter Mondale and John Kerry refused to back the "historic" 2024 Democratic nominee.

And think about this for a moment: During this election cycle, Donald Trump has been compared to Hitler (again) by more than a few in the media in an effort to boost the Democrats, including by the same *Washington Post*, who has offered these Pulitzers going back to the 2016 campaign.

September 2016: Don't Compare Donald Trump to Adolf Hitler. It Belittles Hitler
December 2023: Yes, It's OK to Compare Trump to Hitler
September 2024: Trump Gets Compared with History's Great Villain Because His Rhetoric Is That Bad

But now they won't endorse his opponent?

Is she really *that* bad?

Former editor Marty Baron called the decision "cowardice, with democracy as its casualty."

"Disturbing spinelessness at an institution famed for courage," he added.

Yeah, no bias and hyperbole there whatsoever. This is the same guy who greenlighted the ludicrous *Democracy Dies in Darkness* slogan for the paper right after Trump was inaugurated the first time in early 2017.

Its current editor, Will Lewis, said the reason for the non-endorsement is based on the newspaper "returning to its roots" of not endorsing any presidential candidates. But this explanation simply doesn't cut it. If this was always their intention, why wait until shortly before the election to announce it?

Politico: The *Post*'s Non-Endorsement: Poor Timing, Worse Message
Vanity Fair: "Cowardice": *Washington Post* Blasted for Not Endorsing in 2024
Guardian: The *Washington Post* is a reminder of the dangers of billionaire ownership
New York Post: Watergate Reporters Woodward and Bernstein Calls *Washington Post* Decision to Not Endorse Kamala Harris "Disappointing"

The rest of the media was absolutely convinced the non-endorsement was down to fear of the right, or pressure from above. Clearly, the good people of *WaPo* must be being held hostage either by their own neuroticism or powerful leadership.

But maybe there's another reason why the *Post* endorsement didn't happen. Maybe, *just maybe*, they'd watched Kamala's train wrecks with *60 Minutes*, Fox News, and her town hall on CNN. Even Democrats were horrified with her performances, with former Obama strategist David Axelrod even going so far to call her out for nonanswers by describing them as "word salad city." It's possible, probable even, that the right people at the *Post* decided not to board a sinking ship. However, not everyone at the paper agreed with the decision.

Predictably, several editors and writers at the *Post* announced after the non-endorsement that they were so irate Kamala didn't get an endorsement nobody outside the media bubble cares about (again, because it would be so unsurprising), they were resigning from the publication.

"I cannot sit here any longer on the editorial board and write those editorials while we ourselves have given in to silence. We face a terrible, terrible choice, I believe, a looming autocracy. I don't want to be silent about it. I don't want the *Post* to be silent about it, and the fact that we're not going to endorse is a degree of silence I can't stand," bellowed now-ex-editorial writer David Hoffman while being the least self-aware person on the planet.

Hoffman believes "a looming autocracy" is coming? The country faces a terrible, terrible choice? Does that sound remotely objective to you? Give this guy a show on MSNBC already.

The decision from the Jeff Bezos–owned *Post* came a few days after the *Los Angeles Times*, which has the largest subscription base in Kamala's home state of California, also declined to endorse either of the candidates. In this case, this non-endorsement occurred because the paper's owner, Dr. Patrick Soon-Shiong, publicly said it shouldn't be in the endorsing business. And he's right.

This prompted three editorial board members at the *Los Angeles Times* to resign in disgust, once again showing just how far left a newsroom can become if these "journalists" were *that pissed-off* that their candidate of choice wasn't getting their backing.

But there may have been something else in play here: For several weeks, Donald Trump had been on an upward trajectory in the polls. Almost every major forecaster had him as the favorite to win after somehow trailing Kamala in August and September.

He was tied nationally in the weeks leading up to Election Day. That's a position Trump never came close to achieving in 2016 or 2020. He was ahead in every swing state, albeit narrowly. But again, Trump never led in most swing states in 2016 or 2020 at any time before the election.

So, were the non-endorsements of the *Washington Post* and the *Los Angeles Times* merely hedging moves to avoid publicly backing a losing candidate, one going the wrong way in the polls at the wrong time? It sure seemed like it.

But at the end of the day, the freakout was more important than the lack of endorsements, because what that hysteria demonstrated was that journalists perceive themselves not as objective reporters or even partisan commentators, but as kingmakers. In what way would a bloviating endorsement announcement help persuade anyone who wasn't already on their side? Did they think there were countless Americans out there hovering over whether to choose the alleged democracy-ending candidate but waiting merely for the Kamala pitch from the *Washington Post*?

If these journalists had been living in the real world, they would have understood that the voters Kamala needed to win were the ones least likely to be persuaded by media virtue signaling: the working-class. Kamala had a worse problem regarding another kind of endorsements: from the unions.

Exhibit A: The largest union in the country at 1.3 million members, the Teamsters, of Jimmy Hoffa fame, refused to back her. Internal polling showed Trump up 27 points on Kamala among its rank and file after the same internal polling showed Joe Biden with a majority of support before he dropped out.

Ther reason for the massive flip? Scranton grandpa Biden could appeal to the rank-and-file members. Trump could also appeal to them, being the populist that he is. But Kamala, a San Francisco elitist radical, could not. It was that simple.

The Firefighters Union, which boasts nearly 350,000 members, also rejected supporting her, as did the Arab American PAC, based in the key state of Michigan. And you had to believe rank-and-file of other major unions weren't crazy about her either.

How about the United Auto Workers? Do you think autoworkers like hearing about Kamala-backed electric vehicle mandates that would cost thousands of jobs since electric vehicles don't need as much work to assemble as gas-powered cars?

How about the culinary unions in service-heavy cities like Las Vegas? Trump announced he supports eliminating tax on tips. Kamala followed suit not long after, despite never once talking about such a proposal in her life, in an effort to copy and paste his agenda. Those workers *had* to know it was just another ploy to get elected.

Big picture, you get the point: the backing of unions has always been a slam-dunk for any Democrat. Remember, these are all unions and newspapers who heartedly endorsed Biden, Hillary, and Barack. It was never even a question.

That's not to say some large entities didn't back Harris.

To that end, here's one endorsement that is appropriate for this candidate:

Kamala Harris has a long career in public service, which has given her a keen understanding of how the skilled civil servants who perform the day-to-day work of government are vital to our democracy. She is a powerful voice for workers and their unions, recognizing that taxpayers are better served when the federal workforce is organized and empowered to help agencies meet their important public service missions.

That's the full-throated endorsement from IRS agent union president Doreen Greenwald. Yep. The union, whose members consist of *IRS agents*, loves Kamala! This is basically the last endorsement anyone would covet in this environment, but she got it!

Even the hilarious Kamala Wins! X account bear-hugged the news: "BREAKING: The IRS Union just announced they are endorsing Kamala Harris. Let's go!"

Wow. They actually wrote that! The post, on X alone, received more than 60 million views, and for all the wrong reasons.

So let's unpack some of the endorsements for Kamala:

- IRS union
- Liz Cheney
- Dick Cheney
- Mark Cuban
- The Mooch
- Lincoln Project
- Jennifer Rubin
- Jeff Flake
- Bill Kristol
- Charlie Sykes

- Rick Wilson
- Ana Navarro
- Adam Kinzinger
- Basically everyone at *The Bulwark* podcast
- Fat Joe
- Bad Bunny
- Jimmy Kimmel
- George Clooney
- Former staffers of Mitt Romney
- Former staffers of John McCain
- Former staffers of George W. Bush
- Taylor Swift
- LeBron James
- Cardi B

That's a winning coalition right there. Looks like the 1998 Yankees roster.

Meanwhile, here are some of the names who endorsed Trump:

- Fraternal Order of Police
- National Border Patrol Council
- Elon Musk
- Tulsi Gabbard
- Robert F. Kennedy Jr.
- Joe Rogan
- Megyn Kelly
- Sylvester Stallone
- Dennis Quaid
- Mel Gibson
- James Woods
- Tucker Carlson
- Dana White
- Hulk Hogan

- Kid Rock
- Dr. Phil
- Zachary Levi
- Amber Rose
- Caitlyn Jenner
- Mike Tyson
- Jake Paul
- Buzz Aldrin
- Nick Bosa
- Brittany Mahomes
- Danica Patrick
- 50 Cent

I don't know . . . is it me or are Trump's endorsers, for lack of a better word, cooler?

In the weeks leading up to Election Day, as the Teamsters' internal polling showed massive shifts to Trump, as well as public polling showing the same for Black and Latino voters moving away from Kamala and to Trump, I kept making the same argument on the air during my bullish assessment of Trump's chances:

"Kamala Harris doesn't have the kind of levels of support she needs from union members, how does she win? If she can't run up the score with Black voters and Hispanic voters in cities like Atlanta, Philadelphia, Detroit, how does she win Georgia, Pennsylvania, and Michigan? How does she even win the popular vote?" I asked rhetorically to Larry Kudlow.

After the election, Teamsters President Sean O'Brien revealed that Kamala tried to strongarm an endorsement out of him while refusing to answer questions from the rank and file. Here's what he told Tucker Carlson in December 2024:

> She finally agrees to come after we put pressure on her. Same
> questions, rank-and-file members asking questions, just like

with every other candidate. And they were trying to negotiate with us, she only wants to answer three questions. Like, there are sixteen questions. So she answers three of them, and on the fourth question, one of her operatives or staff slips a note in front of me, "This will be the last question. It was twenty minutes early from the time it was going to end. And so, you're there trying to get our support. And her declaration on the way out was, "I'm going to win with you or without you." She said that out loud.

Who does this fucking lady think she is? If I want support from any organization, I am not gonna point my finger in some-one's face and say, "You better get on board or else."

O'Brien also said that at that moment, he knew she was going to lose. Never eff with the Teamsters.

On the first day of October, five weeks before Election Day, the last big prime-time event featuring the Kamala and Trump camps on the same stage was to take place in New York City.

Tim Walz. JD Vance. The vice presidential debate.

VP showdowns, we were told, never move the needle and are largely forgotten the next day.

This debate, however, would prove to be a major exception.

The VP Debate Reveals
Who's Actually Weird

Trump won't succeed . . . too many Americans would crawl on broken glass to vote against him.

—GEORGE CONWAY

October 1, 2024. New York City. CBS News headquarters.

The vice presidential debate between JD Vance and Goofy Tim Walz was about to begin on CBS. The moderators were Norah O'Donnell, anchor of the *CBS Evening News,* and Margaret Brennan, anchor of *Face the Nation.*

The studio used inside the CBS HQ? The one the network used to tape *Captain Kangaroo* in. And that was only fitting given what we were about to witness.

To this point in the campaign, JD Vance was brutally maligned in the media. He had the lowest favorability ratings of the four candidates in the race. And who had the highest at the time?

You guessed it: Goofy.

But in recent days, the governor had been having some real issues regarding his credibility. As we saw earlier, several news outlets reported he had lied when he said he was in Hong Kong during the Tiananmen Square Massacre when he was actually in a cornfield in Nebraska. And in the only moment when the CBS moderators did their job correctly all night, Margaret Brennan asked the following:

Brennan: *We want to ask you about your leadership qualities, Governor Walz. You said you were in Hong Kong during the deadly Tiananmen Square protest in the spring of 1989. But Minnesota Public Radio and other media outlets are reporting that you actually didn't travel to Asia until August of that year. Can you explain that discrepancy? You have two minutes.*

This is the way he answered a question he *had* to know was coming. From the CBS transcript:

Goofy: *Yeah. Well, and to the folks out there who didn't get at the top of this, look, I grew up in small, rural Nebraska, town of four hundred. Town that you rode your bike with your buddies till the streetlights come on, and I'm proud of that service.*

Concha at home watching: *What? Exactly what does riding bicycles at dusk have to do with the question? And you're proud of what service? Riding a Schwinn?*

Goofy: *I joined the National Guard at seventeen, worked on family farms, and then I used the GI bill to become a teacher. Passionate about it, a young teacher. My first year out, I got the opportunity in the summer of '89 to travel to China, thirty-five years ago, be able to do that. I came back home and then started a program to take young people there. We would take basketball teams, we would take baseball teams, we would take dancers, and we would go back and forth to China. The issue for that was, was to try and learn. Now, look, my community knows who I am. They saw where I was at.*

Concha at home: *What the fuck is he even talking about? We've gone from bikes to basketball and baseball and dance squads traveling to and from a communist adversary?*

Goofy: *They, look, I will be the first to tell you I have poured my heart into my community. I've tried to do the best I can, but I've not been perfect. And I'm a knucklehead at times, but it's always been about that. Those same people elected me to Congress for twelve years. And in Congress I was one of the most bipartisan people. Working on things like farm bills that we got done, working on veterans benefits. And then the people of Minnesota were able to elect me to governor twice. So look, my commitment has been from the beginning, to make sure that I'm there for the people, to make sure that I get this right. I will say more than anything, many times, I will talk a lot. I will get caught up in the rhetoric. But being there, the impact it made, the difference it made in my life. I learned a lot about China. I hear the critiques of this. I would make the case that Donald Trump should have come on one of those trips with us. I guarantee you he wouldn't be praising Xi Jinping about Covid. And I guarantee you he wouldn't start a trade war that he ends up losing. So this is about trying to understand the world. It's about trying to do the best you can for your community, and then it's putting yourself out there and letting your folks understand what it is. My commitment, whether it be through teaching, which I was good at, or whether it was being a good soldier or was being a good member of Congress, those are the things that I think are the values that people care about.*

Again, the question was, Why did you say you were in Hong Kong during the 1989 massacre of pro-democracy protesters in Beijing when you weren't even in the country? Why did you lie about it all of these years?

Brennan: *Governor, just to follow up on that, the question was, can you explain the discrepancy?*

Goofy: *No. All I said on this was, is, I got there that summer and misspoke on this, so I will just, that's what I've said (long pause). So I was in Hong Kong and China during the democracy protest, went in, and from that, I learned a lot of what needed to be in governance.*

Now, this was the biggest takeaway of the night for me: Did he just say that he learned what needed to be in governance by studying . . . *the Chinese government?*

This ought to have been an easy question to answer. Dismiss the date discrepancy as a memory problem, make it clear you take China seriously as a geopolitical and cultural adversary, and don't compliment an authoritarian state. Instead we got Life of Tim. And that concluded the worst 150 seconds any candidate has ever had in any debate, even on the high school level. Meanwhile, JD Vance looked positively comfortable. That's what happens when you're easily the smartest person in the room, moderators included.

Speaking of the moderators, outside of that one benign follow-up by Brennan to Walz after his rambling, incoherent answer, they appeared to have decided the evening was going a bit too well for Vance and began to break out the fact-checks. But Goofy got a pass on this front, while JD certainly did not.

At one point, Vance broached the Springfield, Ohio, migrant crisis after Walz first did in an effort to demonize Trump. Springfield, you recall, was a community overrun by primarily Haitian migrants due to the Biden-Harris open border.

Vance: *Governor Walz brought up the community of Springfield, and he's very worried about the things that I've said in Springfield. Look, in Springfield, Ohio, and in communities all* *across this country, you've got schools that are overwhelmed, you've got hospitals that are overwhelmed, you have got housing that is totally unaffordable because we brought in millions of illegal immigrants to compete with Americans for scarce homes. The people that I'm most worried about in Springfield, Ohio, are the American citizens who have had their lives destroyed by Kamala Harris's open border. It is a disgrace, Tim. And I actually think, I agree with you. I think you want to solve this problem, but I don't think that Kamala Harris does.*

After Walz gave another rambling answer that included quoting the Bible, Brennan jumped in with a fact-check. CBS had assured us before the debate that it would *not* fact-check, of course, but hacks gotta hack.

Brennan: *To clarify for our viewers, Springfield, Ohio, does have a large number of Haitian migrants who have legal status. Temporary protected status. Norah.*

Vance: *Well, Margaret, Margaret, I think it's important because . . .*

Brennan (piously): *Thank you, Senator. We have so much to get to.*

O'Donnell: *We're going to turn out of the economy. Thank you.*

Vance: *Margaret. The rules were that you guys weren't going to fact-check, and since you're fact-checking me, I think it's important to say what's actually going on. So there's an application called the CBP One app where you can go on as an illegal migrant, apply for asylum or apply for parole, and be granted legal status at the wave of a Kamala Harris open-border* *wand. That is not a person coming in, applying for a green card, and waiting for ten years.*

Brennan: *Thank you, Senator.*

Vance: *That is the facilitation of illegal immigration, Margaret, by our own leadership. And Kamala Harris opened up that pathway.*

Brennan (even more piously): *Thank you, Senator, for describing the legal process. We have so much to get to.*

But Vance wouldn't let up, nor should he have. His fact-check of the fact-check was 100 percent correct, which explained why the moderators were in such a damn hurry to move on. They knew their lie was being called out with precision. It was at that moment that they decided to mute his microphones.

Brennan *(with oozing disdain and sarcasm): Gentlemen, the audience can't hear you because your mics are cut. We have so much we want to get to. Thank you for explaining the legal process. Norah?*

What a joke. This was the ABC debate with Trump and Kamala all over again.

Throughout the night, JD had successfully disarmed Goofy with a friendliness and charm few expected him to display.

This was a master class we were witnessing, because JD knew this night with tens of millions watching wasn't about beating Walz in a debate, but winning over undecided and low-propensity voters. To look and sound like a normal, commonsense guy who knows his stuff. And he did so, passing the test with flying colors.

As for Goofy, especially on the optics front, the perpetual split screen showed him looking overwhelmed by Vance's answers. He didn't see this coming. And he couldn't stop saying "Donald Trump." Over and over. He simply didn't make the argument *for* Kamala Harris the same way she failed to make a case for herself in the first and only debate against Trump. In fact, Walz said Trump's name *thirty-eight times* throughout the debate, including seven times in one answer.

The governor's closing statement captured the primary reason why this ticket lost: "Kamala Harris is bringing us a new way forward," he argued. "She's bringing us a politics of joy. She's bringing real solutions for the middle class."

She. Was. Vice. President. For. Three. And. A. Half. Years. What new way forward? What joy? The manufactured variety? The only things she brought to the middle class were higher prices for everything and falling wages. As much as she claimed to be running a joyful campaign, the problem was that her message was nothing but negative. All she could do was explain what she wasn't. There was no positive case for her campaign, and no "way forward" articulated at all. Voters saw through it.

For Vance and Walz, this was the first time many voters got to know them. This was especially true for Walz, who had yet to do a single national TV interview on his own to that point. This hide-and-seek campaign was all by design, of course, because his handlers as well as Kamala's wanted to win this election without saying almost anything outside controlled or friendly settings.

The lack of being tested with anything resembling a tough question showed on that debate stage. Walz often seemed testy, off balance, and lacking confidence in his answers.

Conversely, Vance, who has done dozens of interviews with mostly hostile hosts, came in battle-tested, and the ex-Marine came across as calm and concise.

Postdebate flash polls by CNN and CBS showed that Vance was the big winner.

Vice presidential debates rarely move the needle. This night was absolutely the exception, however. Vance showed he could step in and run the country if called upon. Walz showed he couldn't be trusted to run a bath.

Speaking of 2028, a postelection poll showed Vance leading all challengers with 30 percent of Republican voters backing him. Coming in second was Ron DeSantis at 5 percent and Vivek Ramaswamy at 3 percent.

After Kamala's handpicked running mate embarrassed the ticket (again) during the VP debate, her handlers finally decided to launch a self-described "media blitz" to finally make the sale to voters outside a teleprompter.

You'll never guess how it went.

Media Blitz Causes Kamalacolypse

I think she's going to win, sure. She is just a dynamic speaker.
I mean, the crowd is engaged, the energy is off the charts!
—MARK CUBAN

The time had come for Kamala's friends in legacy media and late-night "comedy" to save her before this election completely slipped away.

Enter Howard Stern.

The year was 1994. I was working making deliveries for a messenger service called Impulse Courier as I tried to break into working for a media organization. For several months before being hired by Time Warner in New York City, I was on the road in the early mornings doing the job like you see so many Amazon drivers do today. It's my DNA: I *must* work or else I risk going insane from anxiety caused by not earning whenever and wherever possible.

At Impulse you could mostly choose when you worked in terms of the time of day. I'm a morning person (as you probably have noticed if you watch *Fox & Friends First*), and my favorite by far was *The Howard Stern Show* on 92.3 K-Rock, out of New York City.

Those who didn't listen to Howard always generalized what the content was. "Oh, he just goes on about lesbian sex and himself" was basically what you heard from the uninformed. Personally, I listened primarily for the interviews, because *nobody* at the time did it better than Howard. He had this unique ability to get celebrities to open up and share details about their lives that you never heard before. Those people would go from guarded and phony to authentic, likable, and fallible in the span of one interview. That version of Stern was Joe Rogan today in the sense that interviews weren't the standard ten minutes, but in fact could go on for well over an hour, even two hours. My driving shifts always breezed by thanks to that morning show.

That Howard Stern no longer exists, however. Instead he's become the embodiment of everything he used to rail against. He's an elitist. He kisses the asses of every celebrity who appears on his show. Worst of all, he's become not just a political activist, but a woke one. Loud and proud.

"I kind of take that as a compliment, that I'm woke," Stern declared on his SiriusXM show in September 2023. "I'll tell you how I feel about it. To me, the opposite of 'woke' is being asleep. And if woke means I can't get behind Trump, which is what I think it means, or that I support people who want to be transgender, or I'm for the vaccine, dude, call me woke as much as you fucking want.

"I'm not for stupidity, you know," he continued. "I ran out Friday morning. I was over at CVS. Thank you, CVS. I went over there, nine a.m. and got myself that new vaccine for Covid. Fucking science. This fucking country is so great. . . . I am woke, motherfucker, and I love it. I want to be awake. I want to read legitimate news sources. Here's how woke I am. I believe the election was not rigged. I am woke. I think that's a compliment."

We'll just leave all of that there. And speaking of Covid, Howard would not leave his home, even for the wedding of one of his closest friends, out of fear of the virus. He wouldn't leave for years. He even would admonish his poor wife, Beth, for going to dinner with friends while he stayed holed up in his mansion. Beth is seventeen years younger than the sixty-nine-year-old Stern and still likes to have a life.

"I'm going crazy with this. My wife yelled at me last night. We got into a fight. You know how paranoid I am about getting Covid? I haven't gotten it, and I'm pretty safe, and I really don't want to get it. . . . Everyone goes, 'Don't worry, it's just a cold for me.' It'll probably be way worse."

He went on this rant in late *2023*, mind you, at least two *years* after 99 percent of the country had returned to normal. And right on cue, three months later, the guy with multiple Covid vaccine shots, the guy who thought he could hide from it forever, contracted Covid-19.

If the old version of Howard had had the opportunity to interview Kamala Harris, there's a good chance he would have asked about her sex life with her husband, Doug Emhoff. And Stern would most certainly have probed about her tawdry relationship with then–San Francisco mayor Willie Brown, who was married and nearly thirty years older than her at the time. It was Brown, who also served for fifteen years as the Speaker of the California State Assembly, who helped get the California political machine behind Harris, who would not have sniffed being San Francisco's district attorney or California attorney general otherwise. She went on to become California's junior senator, eventually a 2019 presidential candidate, and of course Joe Biden's vice president, all without a single notable accomplishment on her résumé besides berating Brett Kavanaugh during his Supreme Court confirmation hearing in 2018.

But this version of Stern wasn't going to touch any of this. So, on a Tuesday in Manhattan, Kamala sat down with the guy I once called the best interviewer in the business.

Now he's the worst. Hands down.

First question from Howard to Kamala: "Do you nap at all?"

Second question (more of a statement): "I'm a huge Prince fan, but I believe that the *Batman* soundtrack was his best work. It was genius. Yes. Think about it. Listen to this. You didn't—it didn't do it for you?"

Third question: "What's Doug into, like, [the band] Cream?"

Fourth question: "Did you ever meet Prince in real life?"

Fifth question (also more of a statement): "As attorney general, it was like you said, 'I don't like talking about myself. It feels—I was raised not to be a narcissist.' And here you're—you know, the other guy is so openly talking about himself. But it's weird. It's odd for you to talk about your accomplishments and sort of congratulate yourself."

Yep. It really did go like this. If I cringed any harder, I'd become a fossil.

Howard proceeded to play a clip of *Saturday Night Live* from the previous weekend to get Kamala's reaction. After she praised Maya Rudolph's impersonation of her, Stern wasn't in agreement. *SNL* should not and absolutely could not serve up even the most benign jokes about Kamala because democracy was at stake, according to him.

"I hate it. I don't want you being made fun of. I—there's too much at stake. I believe the entire future of this country right now," he whined. "I mean as America, land of the free, home of the brave, I think it's literally on the line."

Yup. A "shock jock" actually said that. Imagine the comical series of events that led to Howard Stern to be more piously paranoid than *Kamala Harris*. Even Kamala said lighten up and enjoy the jokes!

I won't bore you with all the rest. It's too painful to relive again as a former superfan of the show. But consider this exchange:

Stern: *The more I think about the people that you're going to have in your cabinet and all this kind of thing, I'm guessing it's going to be Liz Cheney who you appoint, am I correct?*

Harris: *I got to win, Howard. I got to win.*

Stern: *You got to win.*

Harris: *I got to win.*

Stern: *You got to win.*

Oh, good God. It basically mercifully ended with this gem:

Stern: *You'd be a great president. I think you're compassionate. I think you've had all the life experience. I love your experience as a prosecutor. And—and I want to thank you because I know I'm getting the high sign [to wrap the interview]. I want to thank you for all the years of public service. I appreciate anyone who really serves the public and serves them in a—in a way. And I know even as a prosecutor, you got people out of jail who were falsely accused. . . . And I love you as vice president of the United States. And I just want to encourage anyone who thinks similarly to me to vote. And if you don't agree with me, do not vote. I encourage people not to vote who are thinking in a direction of endorsing Vladimir Putin and all that stuff. I hope people get out and vote.*

This was so embarrassing. For all involved. But for all the brown-nosing and all the praise, the interview made no news. Howard seemed to do most of the talking, while Kamala spewed the same word salads around creating "an opportunity economy" while sharing her love for Prince, U2, working at McDonald's, and why Donald Trump was a threat to planet Earth.

On the same day, Kamala ventured to ABC News headquarters for her toughest sit-down yet: With the ladies of *The View*. Actually, "ladies" implies class, so let's scratch that part. But what if I told you in August 2024 that it would be *this* appearance in the friendliest of confines that would effectively end Kamala's chance to be the nation's forty-seventh president?

The question that KO'd Kamala was the top one surrounding her campaign. Sunny Hostin even later called her own question "a layup."

Sunny asked, "If anything, would you have done something differently than President Biden during the past four years?"

Kamala (looking skyward as if she was just asked to explain the atomic theory): "There's not a thing that comes to mind."

Not a thing comes to mind. She called herself the change candidate but also wouldn't change a thing. She was so bad at this. That answer, more than any other Kamala gave throughout her campaign, would resonate the most. And not in a good way. Enter the Ragin' Cajun, James Carville, who ran Bill Clinton's famous 1992 presidential campaign, who was rightly flabbergasted by Kamala's response.

"If this campaign is reducible to one moment, we're in a sixty-five percent wrong-track country, and the country wants something different, and she is asked, as is so often the case in a friendly audience, on *The View*, how would you be different than Biden? That's the one question you exist to answer. That is *it*, that's the money question, that's the one you want. That's the one everybody wants to know the answer to!" Carville exploded on RealClearPolitics.

"And you freeze! Literally, freeze! And say, well, you can't think of anything. Sixty-five percent want something different, we are just not going to give it to them," he continued with his anger clearly showing. "When we go back and history unearths this, it's going to be right there on *The View*. I think her name was Sunny Hostin who asked the question, that's the most devastating answer you can imagine."

Thirty minutes later in the same interview, Kamala wanted a do-over after her advisers clearly got to her during a commercial break, so she shared that one difference between Biden and her is that she is "going to have a Republican in my cabinet."

Uh-huh. Like, I don't know . . . Liz Cheney? George Conway as attorney general? Some "Republicans." That's like King George promoting Benedict Arnold as a concession to America.

Kamala became the first Democrat in history to screw up an interview on *The View*. The irony that Whoopi, Joy, and Sunny helped inadvertently take down her campaign may be the best part of the whole crazy campaign season. Next Harris went to the friendliest of venues: *Late Night with Stephen Colbert* on CBS.

As I observed in the *New York Post*, Colbert's questions predictably centered on how horrible Trump is and the threat he is to the country and democracy. But Colbert also gave Kamala yet another swing at *that* question.

Colbert asked, "What makes you different than the current administration?"

All Kamala could do was flail. "I'm obviously not Joe Biden. I'm not Donald Trump either."

Glad we had that established. But the answer on not being Biden is at odds with what Biden himself said that same week: that his vice president had been involved in every major decision he had made. Indeed the president stressed that the duo were "singing from the same song sheet."

Whoops.

Kamala Harris didn't gain one vote, because the people who watch Colbert or *The View* were already voting for her. But her toughest interview was yet to come, and I'm not being sarcastic this time: a trip to Fox News for a Q&A with Bret Baier. Having watched the *Special Report* anchor for years, I knew one thing for certain: Bret would be prepared and was not going to be toyed with once Kamala began to filibuster or make a misleading argument.

Bret surely knew, for example, that Kamala's go-to when asked about illegal immigration was to blame Trump for opposing a toothless "bipartisan" bill that would not have impacted illegal immigration in any meaningful way. Plus, this was a bill that didn't come about until three years into Biden's presidency, well after the crisis was totally blown open.

> **Baier:** *When you came into office, your administration immediately reversed a number of Trump border policies, most significantly, the policy that required illegal immigrants to be detained through deportation either in the U.S. or in Mexico. And you switched that policy. They were released from custody awaiting trial. So, instead, included in those, were a large number of single men, adult men who went on to commit heinous crimes. So, looking back, do you regret the decision to terminate Remain in Mexico at the beginning of your administration?*

Perfect question. It was specifically focused on the highly effective Remain in Mexico policy, which had been terminated by Biden-Harris. The question also noted that the result of lifting Remain in Mexico was to make American citizens the victims of heinous crimes, including murder and rape. This would be the first time Kamala was asked about Remain in Mexico despite other alleged journalists having had the opportunity to do so.

Her answer, of course, was a nonanswer.

> **Harris:** *At the beginning of our administration, within practically hours of taking the oath, the first bill that we offered Congress, before we worked on infrastructure, before the Inflation Reduction Act, before the CHIPS and Science Act, before any— before the Bipartisan Safer Communities Act, the first bill, practically within hours of taking the oath, was a bill to fix our immigration system.*

Baier jumped in, sensing a dodge. He also knew this answer was coming and quickly noted that this bill, which was basically a pathway to citizenship, wasn't offered to a Democrat-controlled Congress nor Democrat-controlled Senate at the time. Why?

> **Harris:** *We recognized from day one that, to the point of this being your first question, it is a priority for us as a nation and for the American people. And our focus has been on fixing a problem. And from day one then, we have done a number of things, including to address our asylum system and pour—put more resources, getting more judges what we needed to do to tighten up penalties and increase penalties for illegal crossings, what we needed to do to deal with ports—points of entry between border entry points.*

This is all BS, of course. Their focus was on anything but fixing the problem. She, as border czar, visited the border once in the first three and a half years. But the most devastating part of the interview was when Baier correctly broached the fact that Kamala had supported a whole bunch of free stuff for illegals in the country, including illegals in prison, when she ran for president in 2019.

Baier: *When it comes to immigration, you supported allowing immigrants in the country illegally to apply for [a] driver's license, to qualify for free tuition at universities, to be enrolled in free health care. Do you still support those things?*

Harris: *Listen, that was five years ago and I'm very clear that I will follow the law. I have made that statement over and over again and as vice president of the United States, that's exactly what I've done, not to mention before.*

Baier again sees this answer coming and noted that Governor Tim Walz, her running mate, signed a law that allows illegals to get driver's licenses, free college tuition, and free health care.

Baier: *If that's the case, you chose a running mate, Tim Walz, governor of Minnesota, who signed those very things into state law. So do you support that?*

Harris *(blinking at an alarming rate): We are very clear, and I am very clear, as is Tim Walz, that we must support and enforce federal law, and that is exactly what we will do.*

Baier: *Decriminalizing border crossings, like you said in 2019 . . .*

Harris: *I do not believe in decriminalizing border crossings and I've not done that as vice president. I will not do that as president.*

Baier: *So these are evolutions that you've had.*

Evolutions, yes. Because Kamala said this about decriminalizing border crossings in 2019. "Certain communities saw ICE as comparable to the Ku Klux Klan for administering its power in a way that is causing fear and intimidation, particularly among immigrants and specifically among immigrants coming from Mexico and Central America," Harris opined, blanket-accusing ICE, without evidence, of being like a white supremacist group.

Here's what she told MSNBC: "An undocumented immigrant is not a criminal. I know what a criminal looks like who's committing a crime. An undocumented immigrant is not a criminal."

Any questions?

As the interview was winding down, Baier later shared that Kamala's handlers were wildly signaling that he had to end the interview. One could only imagine what *that* panic looked like. Bret also shared that Kamala's team was late for the interview, which made me believe they felt they could shorten the time questions could be asked by doing so. What cowards.

On cue, Bret's line of questioning drew cries of sexism from the left all because he tried to keep the conversation on the rails and not allow her to stall throughout. He did his job. And, by the way, when he interviewed candidate Trump in 2023, he actually interrupted Trump more. So much for the sexism argument. It's his style. Bret correctly doesn't allow a politician to filibuster and control the interview. His method is the way it should be done. Trump called the interview "tough but very fair."

The Fox interview with Kamala drew 7.1 million viewers, making it the most-watched interview she did that election cycle. It even topped *60 Minutes* despite airing at 6 p.m. on a Wednesday while in contrast *60 Minutes* had the benefit of an NFL lead-in on a Sunday evening.

The media blitz was only four days old but already considered a failure. She clearly needed to get every potential voter on board to win this thing. A huge opportunity to do just that and court the large Catholic vote was the legendary Al Smith Dinner in New York City.

The geniuses running her campaign, however, had other ideas.

The "Joy" Candidate
Skips Comedy Night

Hey, calm down. You know what? Victory is in sight. . . . The
opponent is imploding and Harris is doing better than ever.
—JOE SCARBOROUGH

I attended the Alfred E. Smith Memorial Foundation Dinner to cover the event for the *Hill*, a D.C.-based publication, in 2016. That was the first time I saw Donald Trump in person, albeit from afar. The guy filled the room while looking patently comfortable with his opponent, Hillary Clinton, just one seat away from Cardinal Timothy Dolan of the Archdiocese of New York.

Trump got some jeers that night for roasting Hillary more like the way you would hear at a Tom Brady roast from Jeffrey Ross, and less like Don Rickles at the Dean Martin version.

Trump said, "Even tonight, with all of the heated back-and-forth between my opponent and me at the debate last night, we have proven that we can actually be civil with each other. In fact, just before taking the dais, Hillary accidentally bumped into me, and she very civilly said, 'Pardon me.' And I very politely replied, 'Let me talk to you about that after I get into office.'"

See? That's funny.

Trump would go on to defeat Hillary seventeen days later in an election almost no one believed he would win. And a big reason for that was Trump's ability to go into the most deep-blue hostile environments without a second thought.

He even reveled in it.

Fast-forward to October 2024: It was the first Al Smith Dinner in eight years, thanks to Covid. Donald Trump was on board, of course, but his opponent, Kamala Harris, wasn't. Her campaign cited a "scheduling conflict" as the reason for not attending. If you believe that, you also believe that she once worked at a McDonald's.

But more on that later.

Kamala not attending was something that hasn't happened in four decades: a presidential candidate announcing they would not attend this iconic event televised across the country. For more than eighty years the Al Smith Dinner has stood out as a shining evening in an otherwise toxic political culture, raising hundreds of millions of dollars for those less fortunate.

This decision by Kamala, or at least her handlers like David Plouffe and Stephanie Cutter and Jen O'Malley Dillon, came as she had yet to hold even one press conference since becoming the Democratic nominee in late July. In fact, Harris had done fewer than ten interviews to that point since becoming the nominee, while Donald Trump and JD Vance had done nearly *eighty* since becoming the Republican ticket in July 2024. Tim Walz was barely seen, doing fewer interviews than Harris (and for good reason).

My theory as to why she would skip the dinner was simple: she did not want to humanize Donald Trump in any way, shape, or form. And—this is kinda important—there is nothing so cringe as Kamala attempting to do comedy.

Here she is trying to joke about coffee cup lids in 2018:

So you know how those lids on the Starbucks cups, they're white, right? And so, if you wear lipstick, they get all over the lid! (cackle) And so, then I find myself in meetings, if I'm the only woman... and so I keep taking the lid off and having my cup out so that I don't have that big lipstick mark on the lid! (another cackle). So I said, can we do something about the color of the lid? (clapping to herself, extended cackle). So that was that conversation!

Trust me. It's *much* worse with the sound.

That was the fear from the Harris campaign: she would be roasted by Trump with no way to return serve despite having top Hollywood writers on her side. Given her authenticity problem and the fact that she was only exposing herself to the political version of safe spaces, Kamala wasn't going to handle the dinner well.

A Pew Research poll showed that Trump was leading the vice president by 5 points at the time among Catholic voters. Historically, the candidate who wins the Catholic vote wins the presidency. And Kamala not attending was a slap in the face to Catholics.

"I really thought, and I tried to press this with their people. This is literally up her alley," Cardinal Dolan told comedian Jim Gaffigan in an interview before the dinner. "I mean, here you got somebody talking about 'Oh, can't we bring amity and unity?'"

"It's not a campaign speech. It's not a stump speech," the cardinal added. "Now, some candidates might use it for that, but that's not the nature or purpose of the evening either. You know, Ronald Reagan's line [was] the Al Smith Dinner is the rare time where politicians act like statesmen.

"The Al Smith Dinner is not red or blue. It's red, white, and blue. It's all about patriotism, it's all about the country, and it's all about humor," Cardinal Dolan concluded.

It can't be understated enough just how stupid it was for the Obama brain trust running her campaign to sideline her. She may have bombed that night, but at least she wouldn't have insulted Catholics across the country in blowing it off.

But the campaign had an idea for possibly salvaging the evening: to record a video with Kamala in a skit that was sure to win over the crowd!

So again, despite having access to any comedy writer out there from Colbert, Kimmel, or any Hollywood studio, the Harris team basically farted out a video with Kamala and Molly Shannon doing her Mary Catherine Gallagher character that was popular on *Saturday Night Live*, you know . . . when Bill Clinton was president. Oh, and in 2021, Shannon declared Catholicism was a "cancer" that is "destroying the progressive society we built," yet *this* was the person the campaign had perform alongside Kamala in a prerecorded video at the biggest Catholic charity dinner in the country.

Most of you reading this have seen the sketch by now—it was that horrific. And nothing is more cringe than watching a sixty-year-old woman playing a teenager, and I'm not talking about Kamala.

But more importantly, Shannon's unfunny portrayal of a nervous, homely Catholic schoolgirl who routinely wipes her armpits when she's nervous was the real nail in the coffin.

"So tell me something, I'm giving a speech. Do you have some thoughts about what I might say tonight?" Harris asks Mary Catherine in the video.

"Don't lie. Thou shall not bear false witness to thy neighbor," Mary Catherine advises.

"Indeed, especially thy neighbor's election results," Harris replies to crickets in the ballroom.

Who wrote these jokes? Rachel Maddow?

"Does it bother you that that Trump guy insults you all the time?" Mary Catherine asks Kamala.

"Oh Mary Catherine, it's very important to always remember you should never let anyone tell you who you are. You tell them who you are," replies Harris.

Hilarious!

The crowd actually *booed* when the skit was over. Again, this was a charity event in a Democrat stronghold.

Master of Ceremonies Jim Gaffigan, also an *SNL* cast member and no fan of Trump, mocked Kamala's excuse of not appearing.

"You know, this event has been referred to as the Catholic Met Gala. Twenty-two percent of Americans identify as Catholic. Catholics will be a key demographic in every battleground state. I'm sorry, why is Vice President Harris not here?" Gaffigan asked. "I mean, consider this, this is a room full of Catholics and Jews in New York City. This is a layup for the Democratic nominee. She did find time to appear on *The View*, Howard Stern, Colbert—and the longtime staple of campaigning, the *Call Her Daddy* podcast."

It's funny 'cause it's true.

Meanwhile, Trump, the king of all roasters, was *en fuego*. On fire. Here are his top five lines of the evening:

5. "It's really a pleasure to be anywhere in New York without a subpoena for my appearance."

4. "The only piece of advice I would have for Kamala in the event that she wins is not to let her husband Doug anywhere near the nannies."

3. "I used to think the Democrats were crazy for saying men have periods. But then I met Tim Walz."

2. "Tradition holds that I'm supposed to tell a few self-deprecating jokes this evening. So here it goes (pause). Nope. I've got nothing. There's nothing to say."

1. There's a group, White Dudes for Harris. But I'm not worried about it because their wives and their wives' lovers are all voting for me."

The Manhattan crowd loved all of it. The jokes, along with Kamala's cringe video, owned the news cycle the following day.

In 2020, Joe Biden, the pro-choice Catholic, won the Catholic vote by 5 points, 52–47 percent over Trump.

But after Kamala Harris and her team showed a clear disdain for the 52 million Catholic voters in the country, exit polls showed a *23-point swing* to Trump. According to NBC's exit poll, for example, Trump captured 58 percent of U.S. Catholics, while just 40 percent voted for Kamala.

CatholicVote.org president Brian Burch told Fox News that blowing off the Al Smith Dinner was a big mistake.

"She runs for president, and she had a chance to reach out, to extend some kind of compromise, some kind of a gesture even, and she couldn't even do that. She snubbed the Al Smith Dinner," Burch said. "They liked what they heard from President Trump. They liked his attention being paid to record inflation, to the problems at the border, to kind of this anti-woke, let's go back to normal, let's go back to an era in this country where we were proud to be Americans—where boys weren't hanging out in girls' locker rooms, where we didn't have this DEI craziness in our military.

"I think Catholics finally said, you know, I think it's time to take a look at the Republican Party," he added.

Catholics helped deliver the White House back to Donald Trump, all with a huge assist from the brainiacs running Kamala's campaign.

Every presidential hopeful runs to *60 Minutes* in the weeks leading up to the election. Donald Trump wisely sat this one out because the program had proven to be patently dishonest following his last appearance on there in 2020. But Kamala agreed to appear. What happened next is a perfect microcosm of a flawed candidate and a media doing everything to protect her.

60 *Minutes* Sucks

You know who won't get the credit they deserve? Kamala Harris, Nancy Pelosi, Liz Cheney, and tens of millions of women who will be responsible for defeating Trump.

—BILL KRISTOL

Kamala Harris was starting to slip noticeably in the polls as the calendar turned to October 2024. One month earlier, on September 1, she had led Trump in the key battleground states in the RealClear-Politics average after riding high off a free five weeks of over-the-top media adulation. But by October 1, a steady trend toward Trump that had begun after the debate showed no signs of stopping and now he was on top in the polling average.

The Harris campaign could no longer depend on the press to keep her afloat, so the decision was made to appear on the CBS News show *60 Minutes*, which had treated her to a glowing profile earlier in her vice presidency in 2023.

Per the official transcript:

Voice-over: If politics is a game, Kamala Harris has proven herself to be a savvy player, forging a career that has gone from one first to another. The child of an Indian mother and a Jamaican father, she was the first woman district attorney for San Francisco; the first woman to serve as California's attorney general; the first woman of color elected senator from California. And the first woman and woman of color to be elected vice president of the United States.

Bill Whitaker: *Being in that unique position, being that "first"—*

Kamala Harris: *Yeah.*

Bill Whitaker: *Does that bring added pressure?*

Kamala Harris: *No doubt. No doubt. You know, my mother, she would say, "Kamala, you may be the first to do many things. Make sure you're not the last." And among the responsibilities that I carry and maybe impose on myself, that is one of them.*

Oh yeah, this definitely wasn't your mom and dad's *60 Minutes* anymore.

So this time around, the natural choice again would be for the campaign to demand Whitaker do this interview too. And of course, CBS did *exactly* as they were told.

But this time around, Whitaker likely knew that far more eyes and scrutiny were on not only the program's brand, but on him. There were simply too many obvious questions to be asked, and Kamala was known to filibuster like an unprepared sophomore trying to get to a minimum time limit during an oral book report. As a result she would have to face what had been an unknown concept to her to that point: follow-up questions.

That's not to say this interview was necessarily tough. But it was the closest thing to journalism we had seen to this point given the T-ball sessions provided by CNN's Dana Bash and MSNBC's Stephanie Ruhle when they sat down with Kamala.

Needless to say, this interview was a colossal wreck that made the first thirteen minutes of *Saving Private Ryan* seem pleasant in comparison. On October 7, 2024, the pretaped interview aired. And after a Q&A on the Israel-Hamas war in Gaza that would spark major controversy that we'll get to later, Whitaker turned to the economy. And believe me, the transcript does not underscore just how nervous and off-balance Kamala was.

Whitaker: *You want to expand the Child Tax Credit.*

Harris: *Yes, I do.*

Whitaker: *You want to give tax breaks to first-time homebuyers.*

Harris: *Yes.*

Whitaker: *And people starting small businesses.*

Harris: *Correct.*

Whitaker: *But it is estimated by the Nonpartisan Committee for Responsible Federal Budget that your economic plan would add $3 trillion to the federal deficit over the next decade. How are you gonna pay for that?*

Harris: *Okay, so the other econ—economists that have reviewed my plan versus my opponent and determined that my economic plan would strengthen America's economy. His would weaken it.*

Whitaker: *But—*

Harris: *My plan, Bill, if you don't mind, my plan is about saying that when you invest in small businesses, you invest in the middle class, and you strengthen America's economy. Small businesses are part of the backbone of America's economy.*

Whitaker: *But—but pardon me, Madame Vice President, the— the question was, how are you going to pay for it?*

Harris: *Well, one of the things is I'm gonna make sure that the richest among us, who can afford it, pay their fair share in taxes. It is not right that teachers and nurses and firefighters are paying a har—a higher tax rate than billionaires and the biggest corporations.*

Whitaker: *But—but—*

Harris: *And I plan on making that fair.*

Whitaker: *But we're dealing with the real world here.*

(Joe Concha watching this at home on TV): *Fucking finally, someone shows some balls!*

Harris: *But the real world includes—*

Whitaker: *How are you gonna get this through Congress?*

Harris *(eyes dancing while her internal CPU pinwheels, like trying to watch a video on your phone in an area with poor internet): You know, when you talk quietly with a lot of folks in Congress, they know exactly what I'm talking about, 'cause their constituents know exactly what I'm talking about. Their constituents are those firefighters and teachers and nurses. Their constituents are middle-class, hardworking folk.*

Whitaker: *And Congress has shown no inclination to move in your direction.*

(Concha watching at home): *Precisely, my man! Thanks for pointing that out.*

Harris *(now completely flustered)*: *I—I disagree with you.
There are plenty of leaders in Congress who understand and
know that the Trump tax cuts blew up our federal deficit.
None of us, and certainly I cannot afford to be myopic in
terms of how I think about strengthening America's economy.
Lemme tell you something. I am a devout public servant. You
know that. I am also a capitalist. And I know the limitations
of government.*

Wait . . . what is she talking about? She's a capitalist? Did she not
remember how she suggested government price-fixing to stop price-
gouging (that doesn't exist)? Is that a capitalist thing? How about her
proposal to tax *unrealized* capital gains? Not sure that Gordon Gekko
would embrace that. Nor any sane person who invests.

So once again, Kamala couldn't make a basic economic argument.
And when finally confronted with the reality of passing all of these
proposals without any tangible way to pay for them, especially in a
divided government, she imploded into making a ridiculous argument
that Republicans on Capitol Hill were privately telling her they supported her economic proposals. It was almost sad to watch.

Now let's get back to that question on Israel. Again, let's go to the
official transcript released by CBS News:

Whitaker: *We supply Israel with billions of dollars in military
aid, and yet Prime Minister [Benjamin] Netanyahu seems to be
charting his own course. The Biden-Harris administration has
pressed him to agree to a cease-fire. He's resisted. You urged him
not to go into Lebanon. He went in anyway. Does the U.S. have
no sway over Prime Minister Netanyahu?*

Harris: *The work that we do diplomatically with the leadership
of Israel is an ongoing pursuit around making clear our
principles.*

Whitaker: *But it seems that Prime Minister Netanyahu is not listening.*

Harris *(with seemingly no hesitation)*: *We are not gonna stop pursuing what is necessary for the United States to be clear about where we stand on the need for this war to end.*

But hold the phone! That's not the answer *60 Minutes* or CBS decided to show on *Face the Nation* earlier that day. While the sentence "pursuing what is necessary . . . to be clear where we stand on the need" is a roller coaster of discursive nonsense, at least it ends on the clear meaning "the need for this war to end." If that was all she said, it would be a decent *enough* answer, demonstrating a candidate who could almost give a smooth canned response. Except that's not actually all Kamala said, or how she responded to a real question.

Again, this is the answer shown on Sunday night during the final edit to the same exact question:

Harris: *We are not gonna stop pursuing what is necessary for the United States to be clear about where we stand on the need for this war to end.*

And here's the answer that aired earlier that day on *Face the Nation*:

Harris: *Bill, the work that we have done has resulted in a number of movements in that region by Israel that were very much prompted by, or a result of, many things, including our advocacy for what needs to happen in the region.*

But only one answer, the "better" shorter first one, shows up in the transcript. The interview went more than forty-five minutes, yet only twenty-one minutes of the interview survived to make it to air. So where is the full transcript to include the other twenty-five?

Astonished by this crazy discrepancy between the broadcast version and the extended answer, some media outlets, including the Trump campaign, requested that the full transcript to be released, but CBS refused as if, you know . . . *they were hiding something*. Because if they weren't hiding anything, they would release the entire transcript and full video and audio of that interview without hesitation.

"I am willing to bet, Sean, that this controversy goes far beyond *60 Minutes* manipulating one of Kamala Harris's answers to make her look better," I told Sean Hannity the night the scandal broke on his prime-time show. "I'm willing to bet they left several parts out of that interview that did not put her in a good light at all."

I'm still willing to make that bet, to this day: that there were a great many word salads chopped up and left on the cutting-room floor that would have been horrific for the campaign if released. This had nothing to do with "time restraints" but was to cover for Kamala.

For his part, Trump also called on the show to release the transcript. This prompted CBS to respond with a huffy, lawyer-penned defense.

"It begs logic to argue that *60 Minutes* hid the first part of the Vice President's answer to the question," CBS attorney Gayle Sproul wrote in a statement. "It did not. The public is aware of that part of her answer because *60 Minutes* itself publicly distributed it by providing it to *Face the Nation* for promotional purposes and posting it on X and other *60 Minutes*–branded social media for the same reason."

That's great, Gayle. Strong stuff. Nice bit of condescension too.

Now release the fucking transcript.

CBS liked to pretend that its editing was merely to serve the public better with a more newsworthy answer. But as Jeff Blehar at *National Review* pointed out, "it is in fact of great and newsworthy importance if Kamala Harris cannot answer a simple question about her Middle East policy without backfiring like an old gasoline-powered lawn mower."

It's always amusing to check in with CNN's Brian Stelter in these situations. Because this was indefensible, right? It's a simple matter of transparency, which is something all "Senior Media Correspondents" should demand.

"From the network's point of view, caving to Trump's demands to see the unedited interview transcript would break with precedent, suggesting that a powerful politician can bully a news organization into doing whatever he wants," Stelter wrote to mass mockery on X.

Gotta hand it to him, BS never disappoints! Because you see, this is about Trump being a bully more than it is about *60 Minutes* following precedent.

What precedent is that, you ask?

Enter Catherine Herridge, one of the few great investigative journalists left out there. Herridge broke stories for many years on Fox News before signing with CBS in 2019.

"As Trump campaign calls on @60Minutes to release 'full, unedited transcript' of Kamala Harris interview. . . . There is precedent," Herridge posted on X. "When I interviewed then President Trump in July 2020, CBS News posted the interview transcript. This is more complete and NOT the same as a transcript of the edited TV report. It's about transparency and standing behind the integrity of the final edit."

Precisely.

Notably, in 2024, Catherine was laid off by the network because she had the temerity to do actual journalism when it came to the Biden administration. According to her newsletter, CBS News had spiked her exclusive reporting on Hunter Biden and his questionable work with a Chinese energy firm, which they sat on until *after* the 2022 midterms, for example. So the problem goes back quite a while. And it wasn't *just* the *60 Minutes* interview that revealed the ideological rot at the heart of CBS. In the days before that scandal, CBS had publicly excoriated one of its top reporters, Tony Dokoupil, for asking real—but not hard—questions of literary darling Ta-Nehisi Coates about his inane book on Israel-Palestine relations. Dokoupil asked obvious questions like, "Why leave out that Israel is surrounded by countries that want to eliminate it?" And of course, his company threw him under the bus. During an editorial meeting, the head of CBS, Adrienne Roark, claimed that the interview didn't meet "editorial standards." When asked what exactly those standards were, Roark had no answer.

Earlier in the year, a senior director of standards and practices at CBS instructed reporters not to describe Jerusalem—otherwise known as a city in Israel—as being *a city in Israel*.

So perhaps the *60 Minutes* scandal shouldn't have been a surprise. It certainly wasn't one to Trump, who had refused to go on the clearly biased show. After the Kamala scandal broke, Trump decided to take it one step further and announced he would sue CBS for not releasing the transcript.

"News organizations such as CBS have a responsibility to accurately represent the truth of events, not distort an interview to try and make their preferred candidate appear coherent and decisive, which Harris most certainly is not," his attorney wrote. "Due to CBS' actions, the public cannot distinguish which Kamala Harris they are seeing: the candidate or the puppet of a behind-the-scenes editor."

60 Minutes responded and accused Trump of essentially chickening out of the interview, which wasn't the case.

"It's been a tradition for more than half a century that the major party candidates for president sit down with *60 Minutes* in October. In 1968 it was Richard Nixon and Hubert Humphrey. This year, Vice President Kamala Harris and former president Donald Trump accepted our invitation, but unfortunately, last week, Trump canceled," a pious Scott Pelley told viewers.

But beyond the Kamala issues, and beyond all the ridiculous pro-Palestine bias at the network, Trump remembered the way they had treated him in 2020. Why go through the same thing?

Responding to this entirely legitimate criticism, CBS feigned innocence. "Trump said he needed an apology for his interview in 2020. Trump claims correspondent Lesley Stahl said in that interview that Hunter Biden's controversial laptop came from Russia," Pelley also added. "She never said that."

Oh please. That's not what Trump wanted an apology for. He wanted an apology for Lesley Stahl dismissing the laptop as being a major story while refusing to look into it.

To review: during his interview for the program shortly before 2020 election, Trump demanded that *60 Minutes* investigate the laptop and the damning contents on it that could have altered the election, given that Joe Biden, the big guy, may have been compromised by adversaries like China and Russia.

"This is the most important issue in the country right now?" Stahl dismissively asked Trump when he broached the laptop.

"It's a very important issue to find out whether a man's corrupt who's running for president, who's accepted money from China, and Ukraine, and from Russia," Trump retorted. "Take a look at what's going on, Lesley, and you say that shouldn't be discussed? I think it's one of the biggest scandals I've ever seen, and you don't cover it."

"Well, because it can't be verified," Stahl shot back. "I'm telling you—"

"Of course it can be verified," Trump replied, flabbergasted. "Excuse me, Lesley, they found a laptop."

"It can't be verified," Stahl repeated while chuckling.

It couldn't be verified, Lesley, because your crack "investigative newsmagazine" never bothered to verify it.

That's what the apology was for, Scott Pelley.

When all is said and done, no Republican should go on CBS ever again. Between what we witnessed at the vice presidential debate and this *60 Minutes* scandal around the transcript, these are not honest brokers.

This isn't Mike Wallace or Morley Safer.

Margaret Brennan and Norah O'Donnell aren't Walter Cronkite and Roger Mudd.

There is no upside. And fewer and fewer people are watching anymore anyway.

Kamala would continue her "media blitz" through the rest of the week.

It's tough having the name Joe these days. It used to be cool: Joe Namath, Joe Pesci, Joe Torre. But in 2024, poor Joes like me are linked to Joe Biden and Joe Scarborough. But then again, the most popular Joe on the planet may not be former president Joe Biden, but a podcaster named Joe Rogan, who ended up playing a larger role in this election than anyone in resistance legacy media.

Trump Goes for the Bro Vote

First of all, Donald Trump's not going to be elected president. I don't care if he's the nominee, he's not going to be elected president.

—JOHN KASICH

It was January 20, 2020. And the insanely popular podcaster Joe Rogan had made his decision on whom he was endorsing for president:

"I think I'll probably vote for Bernie [Sanders]. Him as a human being, when I was hanging out with him, I believe in him, I like him, I like him a lot," Rogan said at the time.

"Look, you could dig up dirt on every single human being that's ever existed if you catch them in their worst moment and you magnify those moments and you cut out everything else and you only display those worst moments. That said, you can't find very many with Bernie," he added. "He's been insanely consistent his entire life. He's basically been saying the same thing, been for the same thing his whole life. And that in and of itself is a very powerful structure to operate from."

At the time, Bernie was once again causing big headaches within the Democratic Party. Similar to his run in 2016, the self-described democratic socialist was threatening to win the nomination, which sent shivers down the spines of the powers that be in the party, who knew the socialist would likely get smoked in the general election against Trump.

The Vermont senator didn't exactly have the endorsements pouring in, so he gladly embraced Rogan's. But liberals weren't fans of the podcaster and UFC commentator, who at the time was way ahead of the curve when it came to his stance against biological men competing against biological women.

This was unacceptable to the likes of CNN, which described his criticism in a "straight news" story online: "In 2013, [Rogan] questioned—using offensive language—whether a transgender MMA fighter should be able to compete against other women," it reads before quoting Rogan.

"If you want to be a woman in the bedroom and, you know, you want to play house and all of that other shit and you feel like you have, your body is really a woman's body trapped inside a man's frame and so you got a operation, that's all good in the hood," Rogan said. "But you can't fight chicks."

Wait, CNN considered *that* offensive?!

Biden would eventually win the nomination after the competition outside of Bernie (namely Pete Buttigieg, Amy Klobuchar, and Liz Warren) and others all followed the orders from on high and dropped out of the race before Super Tuesday. The binary choice eventually came down to Biden versus Bernie, and just like 2016 and Hillary, the Democratic National Committee and the money were behind the former vice president.

Not long after Biden took office, some entertainers, mainly of the fossil variety like Neil Young, Joni Mitchell, and Crosby, Stills & Nash, began calling for boycotts of Spotify, which pays Rogan big money to broadcast on its platform.

Primary reason? He was allegedly spreading "misinformation" about Covid.

What kind of misinformation, you ask? Here's what CNN described in 2021 as controversial.

"I'm not an anti-vaxx person," Rogan had said, discussing the Covid vaccine. "In fact, I said I believe they're safe and I encourage many people to take them. My parents were vaccinated. I just say I don't think if you're a young healthy person you need it."

In retrospect, was he wrong? Of course not. But in the same CNN article, a Dr. Jonathan Reiner was asked if Rogan was reckless in making such a statement.

"The young are the reservoirs of this virus in our community,"

Reiner said. "They are really powering the spread so the only way to put this virus down once and for all is to immunize."

Are you getting all of this? The argument from Biden, who once declared on CNN that if you get the vaccine, you won't be hospitalized or get sick (false), and the argument from "experts" like Dr. Reiner was that if younger people all get vaccinated, we could "put this virus down once and for all." That proved to not remotely be true.

This sentiment was also echoed by hacks like Rachel Maddow on MSNBC, who is supposed to be the smart one over there.

"A vaccinated person gets exposed to the virus, the virus does not infect them, the virus cannot then use that person to go anywhere else," she insisted to viewers while looking straight into the camera. "It cannot use a vaccinated person as a host to go get more people."

Maddow, of course, never apologized for making such a false statement. Today she gets paid $25 million per year to work one day per week and finishes a distant second to Fox's Sean Hannity in the 9 p.m. eastern hour every Monday night. But, hey, besides that . . .

Rogan is a controversial figure in the eyes of the left because he doesn't bow to the narrative like MSNBC and CNN so reliably do. He is his own man and has his own opinions. These opinions come from doing his own research and drawing his own conclusions. And most of the time, he's proven to be correct.

Fast-forward to 2024: Rogan hadn't endorsed anyone in the presidential race when summer became fall. But there was growing chatter that Donald Trump, reportedly on the advice of his teenage son Barron, was interested in joining Rogan for a marathon interview that usually lasted as long as your average NFL game. And on October 26, just ten days before the election, Trump traveled to Austin, Texas, and did three hours of one of the best interviews you'll ever hear. It was more of a freewheeling conversation than anything else.

My favorite part was Rogan railing against Democrats for being the pro-censorship party, all in the name of stopping the spread of whatever they deemed to be misinformation.

"The rebels are Republicans now, though, like you want to be invisible, you want to be punk rock, you want to like, buck the system? You're a conservative now," Rogan said to Trump. "That's how crazy. And then the liberals are now pro–silencing criticism. They're pro–censorship online. They come in regulating free speech and now regulating the First Amendment. It's bananas to watch."

Elon Musk responded to the viral clip on his social media platform, X, with one word regarding Rogan's sentiment: "Exactly."

"You know they come after their political opponents [too]. I've been investigated more than Alfonse Capone," Trump said to Rogan in response, later adding. "And I've won. I won the big case in Florida. I'm winning the other stuff. You win. But you know what they did? They did something that's only done in third-world countries, they came after their political opponent. I could have put Crooked Hillary in jail. . . ."

Rogan: *Well, not only that, but they're weaponizing it by saying that that's what you are going to do once you get in office.*

Trump (*grinning*): *Of course, yeah. Yeah, isn't it great?*

Rogan: *Ignoring what they're doing right now. It's crazy.*

Trump: *I heard it, somebody was defending me today, says, "No, that's what you're doing to him." They're going, "He's going to put us in jail . . . But that's what you're doing to him." A lot of people say, "Will you do that? Will you do that to them if you win?" The presidency has tremendous power. I could have put Crooked Hillary in jail.*

Rogan: *I respected that you didn't. Because what you said was, "It would be bad for the country."*

Trump: *I couldn't even imagine.*

Now, I can't prove this, but perhaps I was that someone Trump was referring to as defending him. I was on Fox that morning saying the hosts like Joe Scarborough and Mika Brzezinski and the "ladies" of *The View* were hypocrites for saying Trump would throw "journalists" in jail like a crazy dictator would. If anything, I argued, it was Democrats who were literally attempting to jail their opponent in the form of Trump and had actually done so with Steve Bannon and Roger Stone, both of whom served time for no good reason.

My reasoning was simple: Trump was already president and did nothing of the kind. In fact, he was the most accessible president we had ever seen. In 2020 alone, Trump did thirty-five solo press conferences, many of which lasted more than an hour. In 2024, President Biden held (checks notes from the American Presidency Project) none. *Zero.*

This exchange between Trump and Rogan was also hilarious:

Rogan: *I liked how you called [Kim Jong Un] Little Rocket Man.*

Trump: *Yeah . . . I said, "Little Rocket Man, you're going to burn in hell." . . . And then all of a sudden, I got a call and it was from him, meaning his people, they wanted to meet. They wouldn't meet Obama. He tried to meet. They wouldn't even talk to him about it. And I think he expected to go to war. I actually do. And we checked their nuclear stockpile. It is substantial. I got to know him very well. I got to know him better than anybody. Anybody. And I said, "Do you ever do anything else? Why don't you go take it easy and relax? Go to the beach. You have beautiful beaches, nice beachfront property." Kiddingly. I said, "You're always building nuclear [weapons], just relax. You don't have to do it. Let's build some condos on your shoreline." They actually have gorgeous stuff.*

I mean, this is absolute gold. And it's authentic. This isn't the kind of conversation Kamala Harris would have with Oprah, with Dana

Bash on CNN, or with Al Sharpton on MSNBC. Those interviews go maybe twenty minutes. Rogan-Trump went nearly 180.

But here are the most important numbers: on Rogan's YouTube channel alone, the Trump interview was viewed more than 52 million times in just a couple of days, with likely tens of millions more viewing it on Spotify (the company doesn't post view counts).

Meanwhile, on MSNBC's YouTube channel, Kamala's interview with Sharpton was viewed just 267,000 times. As for the standard cable rating, it didn't even win its time slot, finishing second to a *rerun* of *Life, Liberty & Levin* on Fox News, with the Democratic nominee attracting just 652,000 viewers. And in the 25–54 year-old demographic, the Kamala interview attracted just 73,000 viewers, which wouldn't even fill Arrowhead Stadium in Kansas City.

And, by the way, Kamala's team just so happened to make a $500,000 donation to Sharpton's "nonprofit" organization right before the interview. If this happened at Fox, any host would be fired on the spot for this blatant pay-to-play. MSNBC said nothing. But it does beg the question: Did the campaign think Sharpton would have otherwise morphed into Bret Baier and conducted a tough interview? None of it made sense. They just threw money at everything.

Team Kamala, of course, was also invited by Rogan to join his podcast. But since this was the most guarded presidential candidate in history, the campaign demanded that Rogan agree to some ground rules first, including:

1. The interview cannot be more than one hour.

2. Rogan will have to leave Texas and come to Harris at a location of their choosing, something he has never done for anyone.

Not surprisingly, Rogan politely told the campaign to go pound sand on these demands. He wasn't like the resistance media, who agreed to Kamala's terms every time to have time limits and doing pretapes instead of going live to allow for editing after the fact.

The economy and crime and the border and the woke issues like men in women's locker rooms may have decided this election, but that was only part of the equation. From a media strategy perspective, Trump was out there reaching low-propensity voters, younger voters, and Black and Hispanic voters by appearing on different kinds of media outlets, like Elon Musk's X and popular outside-the-box podcasts for conversations that lasted *hours*.

What we're also seeing now are quality investigative reporters simply going to places like Substack and away from corporate media, including actual journalists like Matt Taibbi, Michael Shellenberger, and Catherine Herridge, among many others. That's true journalistic freedom, and it's here to stay.

We see now that Musk's X, which was controlled by the left and literally engaged in censorship, is truly the ultimate free speech platform. It's where people go for their news more than any other place. Overall, according to a November 2024 report from Pew Research, nearly 40 percent of young adults ages 18–29 get their news from news influencers who exist on platforms like X.

Kamala's strategy? She ran to her friends at CNN and CBS and *The View*. And she was reaching a fraction of voters she needed to in the process, especially nonpropensity, younger voters who cut the cord quite some time ago. The Obama team running her campaign were still stuck in a 2012 model. It ain't 2012 anymore.

"You are the media now," Musk declared to his hundreds of millions of followers on X after the election. That post alone was viewed 84 million times. It also caused one of the craziest reactions you'll ever see. The CEO of Axios, Jim VandeHei, completely lost his mind during a speech he gave to the National Press Club after the election.

"Everything we do is under fire. Elon Musk sits on Twitter every day or X today saying like, 'We are the media. You are the media.' My message to Elon Musk is: 'Bullshit! You're not the media!'" a deranged VandeHei exclaimed. "You having a blue check mark, a Twitter handle, and three hundred words of cleverness doesn't make you a reporter!"

OK . . . so would one consider this quality journalism, Jim? Here's what Axios wrote in a straight-news piece on Musk as he was preparing to purchase Twitter in 2022 as one of many examples.

"The goblin [Musk] is serious," wrote Axios "reporter" Felix Salmon.

Why it matters: The world's richest man—someone who used to be compared to Marvel's Iron Man—is increasingly behaving like a movie supervillain, commanding seemingly unlimited resources with which to finance his mischief-making.

Threat level: Musk can be a very dangerous beast when goblin mode is enabled. You're going to hear much more about this bid than you would about a normal proposed M&A transaction, in large part because Twitter is where journalists congregate and do a lot of their work, and they really don't want to be working in Elon Musk's private playpen.

Reality check: Musk claims his offer is "best and final," which will make it easier for Twitter's board to reject.

Of course, Musk would go on to purchase Twitter after his best and final offer was accepted. The new owner would go on to cut 80 percent of Twitter staff who "didn't want to be working in Elon Musk's private playpen." The site has never run better. It is the top news site in 140 countries around the world. X is now the great equalizer. It is now the fact-checkers when we hear BS from our legacy media, and they know it.

Donald Trump was wise to listen to his teenage son. Even Democrats admitted it after the election.

"It turns out that Barron Trump, who looks like a runway model, was telling his father, 'You need to go on podcasts, you need to go on Joe Rogan,'" major Dem donor John Morgan told Kayleigh McEnany on Fox after the election.

"Barron Trump is a lot smarter than everybody in the Harris [campaign]," he added. "If I'm running, I'm going to go on Rogan. I'm living on Fox. That's how you change minds. They played hide the ball, they lost badly, Kamala Harris should go away and never, ever come back."

Ooof.

And he ain't wrong.

When the dust cleared on the failed boycott of Spotify over Joe Rogan a few years ago, not only was he still standing, but thanks to all the ridiculous media coverage, he was propelled into a different stratosphere of popularity and added *2 million subscribers* to the 10 million he already had.

"The problem that I have with misinformation, especially today, is that many of the things that we thought of as misinformation just a short while ago are now accepted as fact," Rogan explained at the time. "Like for instance, eight months ago if you said, 'If you get vaccinated, you could still catch Covid, and you could still spread Covid,' you would be removed from social media."

Rogan would go from the guy who endorsed Bernie Sanders in 2020 to endorsing Trump on the eve of the election.

"The great and powerful Elon Musk. If it wasn't for him we'd be fucked. He makes what I think is the most compelling case for Trump you'll hear, and I agree with him every step of the way," Rogan wrote on X. "For the record, yes, that's an endorsement of Trump. Enjoy the podcast."

Trump now accomplished what would be thought to be impossible entering 2024.

Tulsi Gabbard endorsed him.

Bobby Kennedy Jr. endorsed him.

Elon Musk endorsed him.

Joe Rogan endorsed him.

All never voted for a Republican before.

This perfectly underscored just how diverse the Trump coalition was. As did Trump's choices on *where* to campaign.

Next stop: the World's Most Famous Arena, Madison Square Garden, New York City. And I had a front-row seat to it all.

Live from Madison Square Garden

He's gonna lose. It's not even gonna be that close actually. . . .
I think what actually blew him up was the MSG rally.
—ANTHONY SCARAMUCCI

Madison Square Garden, October 1974. ABC's Howard Cosell is at the mic.

Live, from New York, the city whose landmarks are famous all over the world.

The world's center for shipping, transportation, communications, finance, fashions and above all—entertainment. A city that pulsates always because of the millions of people who live here, work here, visit here. And in the heart of the metropolis, the great arena: Madison Square Garden, which has created and housed so many champions, and which is why tonight from the Garden the most enduring champion of them all, Frank Sinatra, comes to the entire Western Hemisphere live with the Main Event: Frank Sinatra in Concert!

Madison Square Garden, October 13, 1974. Jam-packed with twenty thousand people plus—just people, people from all walks of life, people who are young and people who are old, here to see, hear, pay homage to a man who has bridged four generations and somehow never found a gap.

Hello again everyone, I'm Howard Cosell, and I've been here so many times, and in a curious way, this event, live, with the king of entertainment, carries with it the breathless excitement and anticipation of a heavyweight championship fight!

Celebrities are here in profusion, one after another. Rex Harrison! "Professor Higgins," if you will. Carol Channing—*Hello, Dolly!* Walter Cronkite, "Mr. Believable." And of course, the great romantic hero—Robert Redford. But here, coming through the same tunnel as so many champions have walked before, the great man, Frank Sinatra, who has the phrasing, who has the control, who understands the composers, who knows what losing means—as so many have—who made the great comeback, who now stands still, enduringly, on top of the entertainment world.

Ladies and gentlemen, from here on in, it's Frank Sinatra!

If you've never listened or watched it, please do so. It was originally broadcast on ABC in 1974, hence Cosell's role.

Fifty years later: Madison Square Garden, October 27, 2024. Donald Trump is in the role of Sinatra. It is Trump who has the control, who understands the composers, er, voters; it's he who has the phrasing, who understands what losing means. He's the man on the verge of making the greatest comeback ever.

The Trump campaign was able to provide me a pass into the event, which sold out in less than three hours despite New York being a decidedly liberal city. I was also scheduled to do a hit for Fox News with Jon Scott to talk about the rally from the press riser, which was exciting because I'm usually holed up in my home studio or in a mostly empty studio at Fox News. Field reporting is actually where I got my start on community-access TV in high school.

As I was escorted onto the floor, I was amazed at just how packed the arena, which holds more than twenty thousand people for events like this, was. Not one seat was empty. Usually you can spot a few open at a Rangers or Knicks game because people are in line for the concessions, but for some nefarious reason, Garden management decided the concessions would be closed for hours leading up to Trump's speech, and only when he took the stage would they allow his supporters to get food or something to drink. It was warm that day for late October, and no one was allowed to bring in any beverages like water, so I had to resort to basically begging one concession stand worker to sell me a bottle of water privately.

Donald Trump Jr. was set to speak next around 6:30 but Fox was able to squeeze my hit in between speakers. Here's where my head was at that night just nine days before the election:

"Donald Trump has major momentum right now, Jon. We see it in the polls: Nationally he's now leading, he's never been in that position before [2016 and 2020]. And leading in every swing state in the RealClearPolitics average," I said. "So it's Trump's election to lose at this point, nine days away, Jon."

Jon Scott then pivoted to a poll showing Trump up by 14 points among men, with Kamala up 12 among women.

"Well, she's leading among women as you just showed, Jon, but the problem is that Trump has a huge lead among men," I replied when shown the numbers. "But then the breaking point appears to be that among Black men, particularly young Black men, among Hispanics, among union voters most importantly, the Teamsters, the firefighters unions, refusing to endorse Kamala Harris, that may make the difference. So while Kamala Harris leads among women, it's hard to see where the rest of the coalition comes from to propel her to victory, Jon."

My wife later joked that I sounded awfully confident and how silly I would look if I was wrong. She was right. I was as bullish on Trump's chances as anyone in the media. But it was strictly knowing polling precedent with Trump (always underestimating his support) and the early-vote numbers that showed him leading big in states like Arizona and Nevada, two states Biden apparently won in 2020, that fueled that confidence.

Trump's speech later that night was extremely disciplined. He wasn't going to give his critics any fuel to ignite with victory in his sights. And the crowd loved every minute of not just Trump's speech, but the murderers' row of speakers lined up for the event: Tucker Carlson, Elon Musk, Vivek Ramaswamy, Donald Trump Jr., Melania Trump, Dr. Phil, Dana White, Hulk Hogan, and others. As I told my colleague Aishah Hasnie that night, and which she later shared on-air, it was like the Republican National Convention all over again, except packed into one night instead of spread out over four.

When I exited the building a bit before Trump finished to get ahead of the crowd, it was amazing to see just how many people were watching on the jumbotron outside.

"They could have sold out the place twice," reported the *New York Post*, which estimated an additional twenty thousand supporters were around the arena outside. Tons of Israeli flags were inside and outside the building, and seemingly everyone was wearing some type of Trump gear. As I joked on the air the following day, I hadn't been among that many people so happy since my last spring break in Cancun.

On the way back to New Jersey, I looked at some clips of MSNBC's coverage of the rally.

It was patently despicable, even for them.

"In 1939, more than twenty thousand supporters of a different fascist leader, Adolf Hitler, packed the Garden for a so-called pro-America rally," Jonathan Capehart, who has the audacity to call himself a news anchor and journalist, observed on MSNBC.

"Now, against the backdrop of history, Donald Trump, the man who has threatened to use the military against opponents he calls 'enemies from within,' who has threatened to use the troops to quell what he says are lawless cities and use those troops to carry out mass deportations of immigrants, is once again turning Madison Square

Garden into a staging ground for extremism," Capehart added as the network showed film footage of that 1939 Nazi rally at the Garden.

Goofy Tim Walz also added fuel to this toxic wildfire. "Donald Trump's got this big rally going at Madison Square Garden," he said. "There's a direct parallel to a big rally that happened in the mid-1930s at Madison Square Garden. And don't think that he doesn't know for one second exactly what they're doing there."

As many of you know, MSG has been the longtime home for the New York Knicks and New York Rangers. It has hosted *four* Democratic National Conventions. It's where Marilyn Monroe sang to Jack Kennedy during a birthday celebration in 1962. Two popes have spoken there. The greatest fight of all time, Ali-Frazier I, was held there. I've seen more concerts there than I could count: the Killers, U2, Kiss, Coldplay . . . (Yes, I love Coldplay. Ya got a problem with that?) And I'm pretty sure Billy Joel just lives there at this point.

Supposedly intelligent people know better, of course, but they couldn't help themselves. Cue Hillary Rodham Clinton, who ran to Kaitlan Collins on CNN to repeat this crap narrative anyway a week ahead of the rally.

"One other thing that you'll see next week, Kaitlan, is Trump actually reenacting the Madison Square Garden rally in 1939," Clinton said.

"President Franklin Roosevelt was appalled that neo-Nazis, fascists in America were lining up to essentially pledge their support for the kind of government that they were seeing in Germany," she continued. "So, I don't think we can ignore it."

In a related story, Bill Clinton was nominated in 1992 at the Democratic National Convention that year in (drumroll . . .) Madison. Square. Garden. Hillary was also honored at MSG in 2001 after being sworn into the Senate, and a few years later headlined an event there too. So under this Trump rally narrative, the Clintons are Nazi sympathizers too, I guess.

Since I only saw speeches from 5 p.m. on that evening, I missed some of the lesser-known speakers from earlier in the day. That said, I had zero knowledge of a joke told by comedian Tony Hinchcliffe that was apparently so offensive to many in the media, an argument was being made that the joke could flip voters from Trump to Kamala.

"There's a lot going on. I don't know if you know this, but there's literally a floating island of garbage in the middle of the ocean right now. I think it's called Puerto Rico," deadpanned Hinchcliffe.

Okay. So a guy I've never heard of before made an off-color joke about Puerto Rico's trash problem, which is real and has existed for years with no resolution. It wasn't about the Puerto Rican people, but about the island itself.

> **NPR in 2017:** "Puerto Rico is struggling under the weight of its own garbage... the Environmental Protection Agency says. Most of the island's landfills were filled beyond capacity and nearly half were under orders to close."
>
> ***St. Kitts News Observer***, 2024: "The island's waste management infrastructure is under considerable strain. Many of Puerto Rico's 29 landfills are over capacity and fail to meet U.S. Environmental Protection Agency (EPA) standards. In 2017, the EPA ordered the closure of 13 landfills due to health and environmental risks, but financial constraints have delayed these closures."

Okay, so what exactly is offensive here again? But our media was like a dog chasing a Frisbee on this one. This joke is going to change the race in Kamala's favor!

From CBS News, October 31, 2024:

> A senior Harris campaign official says internal data shows the vice president is winning over battleground voters "who have made up their minds in the last week"—and by a double-digit margin. The campaign, in a phone briefing with reporters, attributed voters' late break to Harris to the negative response to that joke.

What was intended to be a joke about Puerto Rico spawned widespread anger among Latinos, a critical voting bloc. Across battleground states, hundreds have signed up to volunteer for the campaign since Sunday. Celebrities with millions of followers, like Bad Bunny and Jennifer Lopez, publicly announced their support for Harris this past week. Spanish-language newspapers have also endorsed the vice president. Latino organizations have also stepped in to help with field operations to mobilize the undecided voters.

This narrative dominated the news for days. The race was extremely close, the pundits all said in unison as if a memo had gone out, and that one joke was driving enough Puerto Rican American voters into the arms of Kamala and Goofy Tim.

Forget about your grocery bills being too high!

Forget about violent crime increasing in your neighborhood!

Forget about social services being cut to pay for illegals to live in your community! BECAUSE A COMEDIAN YOU'VE NEVER HEARD OF TOLD A BAD JOKE AT A RALLY FOUR HOURS BEFORE TRUMP TOOK THE STAGE!!!!!!

It's just beyond awesome to look back on this now, isn't it?

Thankfully, not everyone bought into this narrative on the left.

"For the media, there was one moment in particular that raised the alarms," Jon Stewart said on his weekly stint as host of *The Daily Show* the following day. "Obviously, in retrospect, having a roast comedian come to a political rally a week before election day and roasting a key demographic—probably not the best decision by the campaign politically. But to be fair, the guy's just really doing what he does. There's something wrong with me. I find that guy very funny. I'm sorry, I don't know what to tell you."

Oh, and how well did Trump end up doing with Latino voters? Glad you asked.

Trump won 46 percent of the Latino vote, marking the highest number for any Republican presidential candidate ever. For context, Trump won 32 percent of the Latino vote in 2020, marking a 14-point jump.

In Florida, which has a heavy Puerto Rican American population, Trump won nearly *60 percent* of Latino ballots. He also took Miami-Dade County, the first Republican presidential candidate to do so in thirty-six years.

This all reminds me of when the Washington Redskins were forced to change their name to the Commanders. This was despite season ticket holders overwhelmingly not wanting the name changed; the owner at the time wasn't in favor of it either.

Nonetheless, the media pushed a narrative in which Native Americans were suddenly outraged over a team name that had existed for many decades, so a pressure campaign, fueled by the media and on social media, was applied to advertising sponsors inside FedEx Field, where the Redskins played their home games. Eventually money talked and the team name was changed, as were one of the most iconic uniforms you'll see in any sport, and the Redskins were no more.

Did a *Washington Post* poll in 2016 show that nearly 9 in 10 Amerindians were *not* offended by the Redskins name? Yup. But media members were offended, especially elite white guys, and that's all that mattered.

Same deal with the Puerto Rico joke: Most Puerto Ricans weren't offended. In fact, more than a few likely agreed with the sentiment. The results of the election help prove that.

In the final week of the campaign it was certain the rhetoric was going to get even uglier, and even more dishonest, from both Democrats and the press alike.

In a potentially disturbing development for the Trump campaign, Kamala was about to unveil a secret weapon to use in making her closing argument of the campaign. And this human weapon of mass destruction was once a high-ranking Republican, no less.

Fry-Cook Trump
Serves Up a Side of Fun

In February 2020, I was asked on the air who I thought would win the election later that year.

"Donald Trump," I immediately replied.

History was my guide on this one. Trump was riding high after a ridiculous impeachment effort by Nancy Pelosi and the Democrats. As you recall, that was the one involving Trump asking Ukraine president Volodymyr Zelenskyy to look into Joe and Hunter Biden's shady business dealings in the country that enriched the Biden family to the tune of millions, all while then Vice President Biden was Obama's point man for all things Ukraine. Joe Biden even got Ukrainian prosecutor Viktor Shokin fired. Shokin was "a threat" to Burisma, the energy company that was paying Hunter Biden, who had zero experience in the energy sector, $1 million per year to sit on its board of directors, according to Hunter's co-director, Devon Archer.

In retrospect, Trump was 100 percent justified in making this request of Zelenskyy. The American public wasn't buying Pelosi's effort here, either, with a *Wall Street Journal* poll taken at the time showing that only 43 percent of voters approved the impeachment of Trump and 49 percent opposed his being removed from office despite most of the media cheering on the trial with breathless coverage.

In February 2020, Trump sat at 46.3 percent approval in the RealClearPolitics average of polls. And you know how polls work with Trump: Take any national number at add five or six points. In February 2012, Barack Obama, for example, sat at 45 percent approval.

He went on to win 303 electoral votes in cruising to victory over Mitt Romney.

Trump also had one the strongest economies any incumbent has ever had going into an election year, while peace was achieved abroad and the border secure, with just 400,651 entering the country illegally that year. Compare that to Biden in 2023, when in November and December alone, more than 430,000 illegals entered the country in just two months, easily eclipsing Trump's number for an entire year.

So that's what I was looking at in February 2020. Covid hadn't shut down the country yet, and nobody could see everything shutting down the way that it did and the economic and emotional hardship that followed. Without the coronavirus, Donald Trump would have breezed to reelection against a hapless Joe Biden, who centered his entire non-campaign as the guy who was going to stop and contain the virus (he didn't).

Considering that 2020 backdrop, could anyone have predicted that McDonald's would play such a huge role in Trump's 2024 victory?

The cover of this book has a photo of Trump on it. And when you ask his supporters where the picture was taken, my unscientific private polling shows about 95 percent could tell you it's Trump working the drive-thru at Mickey D's. Some folks close to me were saying when the cover was being made that we should use the first assassination attempt photo, which may be one of the most iconic shots ever taken. But I pushed for McDonald's, only because that campaign stop perfectly encapsulated Trump's appeal, his humor, and his ability to troll Kamala and the Democrats while sending the media into an absolute tizzy.

To review, Kamala's big applause line (for whatever reason) during her August of joy at rallies was that she once worked at a McDonald's. This was the Coconut Queen's attempt to appeal to working-class voters and make herself more relatable. But Trump—along with many others—began questioning if she was *ever* employed there.

And the reasons for the skepticism were solid:

1. Kamala Harris didn't list her McDonald's job on a law clerk application.

2. Not one person has come forward on record to say, "Oh, yeah, I remember working with her there." Not a coworker, not a manager. If you worked with a future VP at McDonald's once, wouldn't you kinda remember that and want to share that factoid?

3. Kamala wrote two memoirs on every aspect of her life and didn't once mention working there, nor did any third-party biographies written about her.

4. When she ran for president in 2019, she didn't once mention working there, despite being on the campaign trail for nearly ten months.

5. She never once mentioned working there as vice president until she became the nominee.

6. McDonald's could not confirm her employment.

7. The Harris campaign kept changing its story. They went from originally saying that she worked at McDonald's to pay her way through college. Then they said she just needed some extra spending money.

Per left-leaning fact-checker Snopes:

Harris has made this claim repeatedly over the years, and multiple reputable news outlets have reported on the story. But, aside from Harris' testimony itself, there is no evidence (such as a photo, employment record or confirmation from a friend or family member) to independently verify the claim. We've reached out to Harris' campaign and McDonald's and we'll update this report when, or if, we learn more.

Now let's compare this to Barack Obama sharing during his presidential run that he worked at Baskin-Robbins. He knew the address. He had photos. The manager confirmed his employment there.

None of this happened with Kamala's claim.

No matter. Our pathetic media was on a mission to absolutely insist she worked there, and Trump was wrong to question it. Check out these headlines:

MSNBC: Trump's McDonald's Photo-Op Was as Condescending as It Was Ironic: The former president's long record of opposing labor protections and stiffing working class contractors made his play-acting as a low-wage worker seem even sillier.
New York Times: Kamala Harris and McDonald's: A College Job, and a Trump Attack: Donald Trump has claimed without evidence that Ms. Harris never worked at the fast-food chain.
Rolling Stone: Trump Makes Fries at McDonald's in Bizarre Attempt to Troll Harris.

But here was the very best one:

"Rumors Have Been Circulating on Social Media That Trump's Visit to McDonald's Was 'Staged,'" wrote the geniuses at *Newsweek*.

Get out of here! Are you saying that Trump wasn't *actually hired* to be the fries guy and work the drive-through? Classic mainstream media, fact-checking a Republican joke and naively supporting an unprovable Democrat PR story.

The *Washington Post* also beclowned themselves with gotcha reporting that the restaurant was closed to the public (you don't say) and that customers were screened beforehand . . . because it would have totally been a great idea to have Trump work at a random McDonald's open to the public after nearly being assassinated twice.

Goofy Tim Walz and the unbearable AOC also entered the conversation by accusing Trump of causing an *E. coli* outbreak that was reported (checks notes) at other locations nowhere near the one Trump was at in Reading, Pennsylvania.

"Do you notice a lot of people got sick after he worked at McDonald's?" Walz asked.

"Oh, yeah, they showed the *E. coli* outbreak," Ocasio-Cortez replied. "That man stuck his hands in the fries, and McDonald's had *E.coli* like the next day!"

Apparently the only difference between genius and stupidity is that genius has its limits.

But give Van Jones over on CNN credit. He read the room or, in this case, the drive-through, correctly.

"I think it's brilliant. I think it's brilliant," Jones said. "I think we've got to acknowledge that this guy is beating the pants off of us with these so-called publicity stunts. It gets into everybody's feeds and people who are not looking at politics will look at that."

"If we have more fun, if the Democratic Party is a party of fun, people will join it. We should be doing crazy stuff, too."

Bingo. Because as I said on Fox at the time, you know who has the winning campaign by who's having the most fun. Trump clearly was at this point.

"WHEN I'M PRESIDENT THE MCDONALD'S ICE CREAM MACHINES WILL WORK GREAT AGAIN!" Trump wrote on X while showing a photo of a smiling Biden holding a McDonald's ice cream cone while wearing a Trump hat.

At another point, Trump declared, "I've now worked for fifteen minutes more than Kamala at McDonald's."

See, that's funny. And he did it on Kamala's sixtieth birthday, no less.

"I've really wanted to do this all my life. And now I'm going to do it because she didn't do it," he added with a smile.

He once again showed that, despite being a billionaire, he was as relatable as any candidate in history.

"Can you believe this? Look at this guy, he's a MAGA guy all the way," Trump told one customer, a father, with his wife and kids in the car. "What a good-looking family—how did you produce those good-looking kids?"

"The food is all on Trump. It's going to be the best—I made it myself. This is fun, I could do this all day—I like this job," he chuckled.

Think back to 2020 at this time. Trump was in the hospital with Covid to start that October. The campaign couldn't do stops like McDonald's or anything fun, it seemed. Trump trailed Biden in the polls. His speeches had passion but were more brooding, more angry.

Not this time. He was confident. He was having a blast, perhaps appreciative that this would be his last campaign. His internals showed him winning easily. He could do no wrong despite what the media was saying. It was Kamala's campaign that was one of anger. She *definitely* wasn't having fun.

The McDonald's successful stunt dominated the news cycle for the better part of three days. The photo you see on the cover of this book was *everywhere*. Trump's campaign knew exactly what was working while Kamala's comrades were living in the past.

"Where she's doing the big speech or having the big debate, the conventional warfare, traditional campaign tactics, Donald Trump goes to the McDonald's drive-through," explained chief pollster Tony Fabrizio to *Politico*. "But in the year 2024, when we're all living on our phones, a big speech at the Ellipse vs. Trump at the drive-through, which is going to break through?"

That's the best analysis about messaging and media I heard during this campaign.

For days after, on the rare occasion that Kamala took questions from reporters, she was asked if she worked at McDonald's. The fact that this was the focus less than ten days from the election was not good for Kamala's campaign, which was going backward in most polls at the worst possible time.

Well, check that. There was one poll out of Iowa and thirteen keys that said she was headed to victory after all.

Gold Standard Polls

America, it will all be okay. Ms. Harris will be elected the next president of the United States. Of this, I am certain.

—JAMES CARVILLE

Her polls were called the "gold standard."

Ann Selzer. The biggest legend, we were told by so many political pundits, to hail from the state of Iowa since Cloris Leachman. And every four years, her Iowa poll was arguably the most anticipated of the election season.

It was just two days before Election Day when the Selzer poll was released. It set off an earthquake that stunned the Trump campaign while serving as a defibrillator for Kamala's.

Harris +3.

In Iowa.

"Impossible," I said on Fox after it was released. "I cannot wait to come back on here the day after the election to dunk on this poll for being so wrong. Save the tape."

My questioning of this poll was rooted in simple logic and numbers.

1. Trump won the state by about 10 points in 2016 and 9 points in 2020. So now we were supposed to believe Kamala Harris had flipped Iowa by 12–13 points?

2. Registered Democrats made up only 29 percent of the Iowa electorate.

3. Registered Republicans outnumbered Democrats in the state by 143,000.

4. Kamala's internals, if they were remotely near Selzer's result, would have sent her to campaign at least once there.

5. Emerson College released a poll earlier that day showing Trump up by 10 in Iowa.

6. It's freaking *Iowa*.

7. This is Kamala Harris we're talking about.

Selzer joined Mark Halperin on his *2Way* YouTube show to discuss the result. This is where I became 1000 percent confident that she was either compromised here or simply inept.

"What does the *R* represent and the *D* represent?" Selzer asked when shown what her crosstabs looked like by Halperin.

Gee. I'm not a pollster, nor is my third grader, but I'm certain even he knows that *R* stands for Republicans and *D* stands for Democrats.

She also went on MSNBC to share not so much what the data showed her, but to hold forth on her own personal feelings on what may motivate voters.

"Our consensus from the reporters who work this beat is that the abortion ban went into effect this past summer," Selzer said. "I think it has gotten people interested in voting."

Oh, we're thinking now? When Joe Biden was on the ticket, Trump was beating him by 18 points in Iowa in her own poll in June. Biden is pro-choice. Kamala is pro-choice. But somehow, because she's a woman, she's flipping the race from where it was with Biden in . . . by 21 points in a decidedly red state?

"It is incredibly gutsy to release this poll. It won't put Harris ahead in our forecast because there was also another Iowa poll out today that was good for Trump. But wouldn't want to play poker against Ann Selzer," warned Nate Silver, who had Kamala winning this election just like he had Hillary winning in 2016.

Maybe, I don't know, we all stop listening to this guy?

"If this is accurate, and if anybody is accurate, it's likely to be Ann Selzer in the Iowa poll. If this is accurate, it implies that Harris might be winning Iowa," MSNBC's Rachel Maddow swooned.

Selzer would go on to say that she was seeing fewer lawn signs for Trump than she did in 2020, providing more sciencey stuff right there.

The betting markets, where Trump was leading, tumbled on the news of this poll. Champagne corks were likely flying around MSNBC and CNN headquarters. If Kamala wins Iowa, that means she'll take every swing state, we heard. She may even win Kansas and Texas too!

Uh-huh . . .

By around 10 p.m. eastern on election night, we had our answer as to whether the Selzer gold standard was still the gold standard. Trump won the state by 13 *points*, the largest margin for any candidate since 1972. Ann was only off by (checks math) 16 points. No biggie.

"Who exactly did she poll for this? Did she only talk to MSNBC viewers?" a schadenfreude-filled Joe Concha asked on *Fox & Friends First* the next morning.

A few days later, Ann Selzer announced she was retiring from polling.

"Would I have liked to make this announcement after a final poll aligned with Election Day results? Of course. It's ironic that it's just the opposite," she said in an op-ed.

"In response to a critique that I 'manipulated' the data, or had been paid (by some anonymous source, presumably on the Democratic side), or that I was exercising psyops or some sort of voter suppression: I told more than one news outlet that the findings from this last poll could actually energize and activate Republican voters who thought they would likely coast to victory," she added.

"Maybe that's what happened."

Oh, okay. So you're saying that your poll may have been accurate, but it galvanized Republican voters to go to the polls who otherwise would have stayed home to the tune of flipping the result by 16 points? Right, because Republicans are keeping up with Ann Selzer's poll results just that closely.

Trump, for his part, called for an investigation.

"A totally Fake poll that caused great distrust and uncertainty at a very critical time. She knew exactly what she was doing. Thank you to the GREAT PEOPLE OF IOWA for giving me such a record breaking vote, despite possible ELECTION FRAUD by Ann Selzer and the now discredited 'newspaper' for which she works. An investigation is fully called for!" Trump wrote on Truth Social. He would also announce in December 2024 that he was suing her and her polling firm, along with *Des Moines Register* itself, alleging "election interference."

Allan Lichtman's "13 keys" wasn't much better. This guy, who clearly hates Trump, had Kamala winning thanks to 13 data points that he believed were foolproof. His problem was that the conclusions he was entering into his model were flawed and likely the result of personal bias.

On the economy, for example, he gave the nod to Harris because she was essentially the incumbent, and Lichtman believed the economy was a plus-positive for her instead of a negative. He somehow argued this despite every poll showing voters trusted Trump on the economy, felt the economy was better under Trump, and a solid majority of voters saying they were worse off economically than they were five years ago.

Here are some others he got wrong: "Third-Party Key 4: In recognition of his fading support, Robert F. Kennedy Jr. suspended his campaign. His endorsement of Donald Trump does not impact this key."

Oh, that just ain't true. Bobby's endorsement of Trump and campaigning with him made a real difference in broadening Trump's coalition.

Next up: "Long-Term Economy Key 6: Real per-capita growth

during the Biden term far exceeds the average of the previous two presidential terms."

Really, Allan? Inflation averaged more than 6 percent during Biden-Harris. Prices for everyday items are still far too high for many folks, and the cost is still increasing. Wages aren't keeping up with inflation. The federal deficit is easily at an all-time high as spending spirals out of control. Interest rates still are scaring potential homeowners from pulling the trigger. Voters blamed Biden-Harris for all of this and voted against the latter and in favor of Trump.

Next Lichtman pivoted to war. "Foreign/Military Success Key 11: President Biden and Biden alone forged the coalition of the West that kept Putin from conquering Ukraine and then undermining America's national security by threatening its NATO allies. Biden's initiatives will go down in history as an extraordinary presidential achievement."

You're kidding, right? Polls at the time showed that a majority of Americans felt Congress should not authorize additional funding to support Ukraine. Military success was what we had under Trump. We didn't have the disastrous Afghanistan withdrawal. Russia didn't invade Ukraine. Hamas didn't pull off an October 7 attack in Israel. Iran proxies weren't firing at our servicemen and women on a daily basis. China wasn't so aggressive in its posture against Taiwan. Trump destroyed ISIS and tamed North Korea.

Allan Lichtman ignored all of this.

But this was my favorite key conclusion: "Challenger Charisma Key 13: As explained, Trump does not fit the criteria of a once-in-a-generation, broadly appealing, transformational candidate like Franklin D. Roosevelt or Ronald Reagan."

What? Trump is the very essence of a once-in-a-generation, broadly appealing, transformation candidate. Even Democrats would admit that.

Lichtman melted down after the election. He announced he was leaving X, only to come back. And he still insisted in interviews that he wasn't wrong. Even the left destroyed him. Check out this exchange on

Piers Morgan's show between Lichtman and fellow liberal Cenk Uygur of the not-so-young-anymore Young Turks.

"Look, I debated Professor Lichtman before. I told him his theories about the keys are absurd. I was right. He was wrong. I said he'd lose his keys," Uygur declared.

"No, you were not right, and I was not wrong!" Lichtman interrupted while ignoring reality. "And that's a cheap shot. And I will not stand for it."

"Who won, brother? Who won?" Uygur repeated.

"You should not be taking cheap shots at me! You want to make your point, make your point. Don't make it personal!" Lichtman screamed back.

"You live in a total world of denial," Uygur reminded him. "You're just so deluded . . ."

"Oh, right, I've only been a professor for fifty-one years, published thirteen books," Lichtman retorted, as if that had anything to do with anything. "How many books have you published then? No, because you're personally attacking me again. Say whatever you want, but I'm not going to stand for personal attacks."

"But brother, you got it wrong! You were preposterously stupidly wrong!" Uygur yelled back.

"I will not sit here and stand for personal attacks, for blasphemy against me. You don't need to do that," Lichtman said.

"Blasphemy against you?" Uygur shot back. "Who the hell are you? Are you Jesus Christ, you loser?"

I mean, it doesn't get more delicious than that. But don't worry about Lichtman. He and his stupid keys will be embraced by the media again in 2028.

In the end, most of the pollsters didn't understand the very electorate they were polling, just as the media doesn't understand many of its potential viewers in the flyover states.

Impeachments didn't stop Trump.

Indictments didn't stop Trump.

Assassins didn't stop Trump.

The media didn't stop Trump.

And the polls, which underestimated his support wildly for the third straight election, didn't stop Trump.

Jon Stewart, the first major liberal to publicly state that he believed Covid came from a lab that literally studies coronaviruses in Wuhan, nailed it once again when it came to pollster performance.

"Our time is running out," he said on Election Night as Trump was headed to victory. "I do want to very quickly send a quick message to all the pollsters, the election pollsters, um, 'Blow me.'

"I don't ever want to fucking hear from you again. Ever. I don't ever want to hear, "We've corrected for the overcorrection video with the voters!' You don't know shit about shit, and I don't care for you," he continued. "We'll figure it out next time. Oh, we were in the margin of 'Blow Me.'

"Look, look, look. Here's the thing. Well, here's what we know, is that we don't really know anything and that we're going to come out of this election, and we're going to make all kinds of pronouncements about what this country is and what this world is. And the truth is, we're not really going to know shit. And we're going to make it seem like this is the finality of our civilization. We're all going to have to wake up tomorrow morning and work like hell to move the world to the place that we prefer it to be. And I just want to point out, just as a matter of perspective, that the lessons that our pundits take away from these results that they will pronounce with certainty will be wrong."

Amen again.

Heading into Election Day, Trump had Elon Musk and Bobby Kennedy Jr. and Tulsi Gabbard and Joe Rogan in his corner.

But whether it was intentional or not, he also had an unlikely ally in the form of one Joseph Robinette Biden.

Sleepy Joe Jumps
on the Trump Train

I think President Trump's time has passed him by. I think what's the most important thing for me is that we have a candidate who can actually win.

—JOHN CORNYN

It was an odd and awkward Twitter post to absorb: the sitting vice president, Joe Biden, sharing a photo of a BFF (best friends forever) bracelet between him and then-president Barack Obama.

As I said on Fox at the time, "Real men, at least the ones I know, *do not* remotely do anything like this with our friends." And the guess here was that Biden only shared this bracelet in 2019 because he was running for president and wanted to remind everyone that he was joined at the hip (in this case, the wrist) with Obama, who was still popular with the base.

In a related story, it should be noted that the first sentence of my first book, *Come On, Man: The Truth About Joe Biden's Terrible, Horrible, No-Good, Very Bad Presidency*, was this quote, reportedly from Obama himself: "Never underestimate Joe Biden's ability to fuck things up."

Just going to leave that one there.

So when we were continually told that Biden and his vice president were also BFFs, it was easy to be skeptical of their relationship. After all, Kamala Harris kinda did infer that Joe was a racist during the first primary debate of the 2020 campaign. And though in public everyone seemed to have made up, something tells me that fake "Dr." Jill Biden was not happy with that attack.

"The one thing you cannot say about Joe is that he's a racist. I mean, he got into politics because of his commitment to civil rights. And then to be elected with Barack Obama, and then someone is saying, you know, you're a racist?" she asked CNN while clearly pissed.

"The American people know Joe Biden. They know his values. They know what he stands for. And they didn't buy it," she added.

Joe Biden agreed with that sentiment while noting that he was taken aback by Kamala's broadside. "I've been surprised, not about the attacks, but I've been surprised at the intentions sometimes of the attacks, coming from people who know me," the former vice president said.

After that debate, Jill Biden reportedly wasn't as measured with her words. According to multiple reports, on a call with supporters she said: "With what he cares about, what he fights for, what he's committed to, you get up there and call him a racist without basis? Go fuck yourself!"

Kamala would drop out a few months later, after Democrat voters got to know her. Biden would go on to capture the nomination and choose her to be his veep, only because he promised to select a woman of color.

In other words, it was the political equivalent of an arranged marriage.

But Dr. Jill apparently never completely forgave Kamala for the comment. As for Joe, his oftentimes almost-vacant daily presidential schedule released to the public included a weekly lunch with his vice president.

"[Like] Barack and I, we have lunch alone once a week. . . . That's the deal when we're both in country, which we'll be for a while because of Covid, and I see her all the time," Biden announced in early 2021.

But there's little evidence that these lunches actually happened on any consistent basis. For example, according to the *New York Post*,

"Records of the president's public schedule show that in 2022, Biden and Harris were scheduled for lunch in the private dining room on just Feb. 8 and March 30."

So why have it on the schedule every week? To follow the same guiding principle that embodied this entire cartoonish administration: perception.

I always try to make this point on the air when it comes to talking about any politician, regardless of party: never take anyone at their word; always judge them on their actions. Donald Trump, for example, is a man of action. He gets things done. Biden and Harris, conversely, were mostly talk, and the only actions they'll be remembered for in the sorriest of legacies were reversing Trump's actions on the border, reckless spending, woke policies, and building a 2024 campaign that became the political equivalent of the *Hindenburg*: a lot of hot air destined for disaster.

The relationship between Biden and Harris only got worse when Joe was driven off the ticket kicking and screaming. My educated theory is that even with his mind starting to go, he knew that he was still a much better candidate than she was. He still wouldn't have won, because the Biden-Harris brand was the Enron of politics and Trump ran a masterful campaign, but Biden may have done better in states like Pennsylvania and Michigan than Kamala because of his strong union ties and because he doesn't come off as phony on the lunch bucket front as she does.

The first indication that Joe and Jill were not on board with Kamala-Walz came at the Democratic National Convention in Chicago. This was the ultimate insult: Joe was given a speaking spot on the first night of the convention, Monday, but the 10:30 p.m. spot eventually got bumped to 11:30 as the convention dragged on, functionally burying him to speaking very late at night. Even Nate Silver saw through it. "You've gotta be pretty naive to think the prolonged DNC tonight is for any reason other than diminishing Biden's visibility," he wrote, noting that the late slot hid Biden away from the largely East Coast–based media. A Biden aide mourned anonymously in a text to a journalist, "This is awful. He literally set up a campaign and handed it over to them—do they have to cut him out of prime time?"

Biden was then told to leave right after leaving the stage. If I'm him, I'm beyond aggrieved that I'm being disrespected like that. But Democrats wanted to pretend that Kamala had just shown up five minutes after Biden dropped out as a fresh face with new ideas, and having old Joe around as a reminder to viewers she was still his vice president just wasn't going to happen.

As the election drew closer, it was clear Biden wasn't going to be tapped to campaign for or with Kamala in any capacity. *Politico* on October 20: "It's a remarkably diminished position in the 2024 campaign for a president who until just a few months ago was at the top of the Democratic ticket. It comes as Harris is trying to convince voters in the final days before the election that she does not represent a second Biden term and instead is a candidate of change. Harris aides believe that message could be undermined by images of her on the campaign trail with the president."

Kamala also was starting to push the message that she was going to be a vast improvement over her boss, which must have rubbed him and the first lady the wrong way.

"Let me be very clear: my presidency will not be a continuation of Joe Biden's presidency," Harris told Bret Baier on Fox News that same week. Yep, the same VP who said Bidenomics was working great did not want the awesomeness to continue. Go figure.

Joe Biden put up with it, probably silently fuming that his plan to totter on for another four years as the world's most powerful man was being eclipsed by his dilettante VP.

But it was on September 11, 2024, that the dam began to break. Joe Biden was in Shanksville, Pennsylvania, where United Airlines Flight 93 crashed on 9/11 after passengers heroically stormed the cockpit hijacked by al-Qaeda terrorists who had intentions of crashing it into the White House or the U.S. Capitol Building. Biden visited a local fire department that day after a memorial to mark the twenty-third anniversary of the attack.

At one point Biden engaged with a Trump supporter in the department, who was wearing a Trump 2024 hat at the time. Biden smiled and borrowed the hat and put it on, faced reporters covering the event, and smiled from ear to ear.

The moment went viral, and came just one day after Trump said the following in his debate with Kamala Harris: "He got 14 million votes, and they threw him out of office. And you know what? I'll give you a little secret. He hates her. He can't stand her," Trump said, making Biden's decision and timing to put on a Trump hat that much more curious.

Then this happened on October 4, one month and one day before the election. Kamala Harris was holding a rally in the crucial state of Michigan. The time was 2:04 p.m. eastern. Several news outlets had preempted regular programming to carry her remarks live.

At that moment, and for the first time in his presidency, Joe Biden decided to make the short walk from the Oval Office to the James S. Brady Press Briefing room to take questions from reporters who were there for the White House press briefing. And on cue, any network carrying the Coconut Queen's rally was obviously forced to dump out and switch to Biden, given how rare the moment was for this president.

Now remember: Kamala was also in the middle of her media blitz, where she had emphasized that she was *not* Joe Biden and that his policies and worldview were quite different from hers. Granted, she had enormous difficulty stating exactly what those differences were, but whatever: it was still a rejection of the president, and Biden seemed to have had enough.

Reporter: *There have obviously been a number of crises that the country has been facing over the past several days with the hurricane, with the port strike, with the situation in the Middle East. Can you talk about how your vice president, who is running*

*for the presidency, has worked on these crises and what role she
has played over the past several days?*

Biden: *Well, I'm in constant contact with her. She's aware, we're
all singing from the same song sheet. She helped pass all the laws
that are being employed. Now, she was a major player in everything
we've done, including passage of the legislation which we were told
we could never pass. And so, she's been—and her staff is interlocked
with mine, in terms of all the things we're doing.*

Holy crap. Not only did he preempt her rally's news coverage, but
he directly attached her to everything that the administration had done
over the past three and a half years. They're in constant contact. They're
singing from the same sheet of music. She's a major player in Biden-
Harris. She got legislation like the destructive Inflation Reduction Act
over the finish line. They're interlocked!

Another reporter: "Do you want to reconsider dropping out of the
race?"

Biden (jokingly before leaving the room): "I'm back in!"

He sure was. As the Trump War Room X account noted, "Biden is
Kamala. Kamala is Biden."

Then there was the aftermath of Hurricane Helene, which again
showed Joe's possible disdain for Kamala. If you recall, Florida
governor Ron DeSantis had done an exceptional job (again) in the
hurricane's aftermath in providing his residents with an army of re-
sponders to get them the help and shelter needed while getting things
back to normal as quickly as possible. I'm not sure there's ever been a
governor who has responded to natural disasters more efficiently and
effectively.

But Kamala's handlers, for whatever reason, decided they wanted
to share in the credit for DeSantis's successful efforts, so they tried to
arrange a phone call with him in what was clearly a political stunt to
make her look presidential. When there was no response from DeSantis,

Kamala attacked him. DeSantis said he didn't even know she called. But even if he did, he likely knew he was being used as a prop and simply wanted to concentrate on the task at hand. Besides, the governor was already in regular contact with President Biden.

"You know, moments of crisis, if nothing else, should really be the moment that anyone who calls themselves a leader says they're gonna put politics aside and put the people first," a flustered Kamala told reporters after being unnoticed by DeSantis.

"And playing political games at this moment in these crisis situations, these are the height of the emergency situations, it's just utterly irresponsible, and it is selfish, and it is about political gamesmanship instead of doing the job that you took an oath to do, which is to put the people first," she added.

During a Fox appearance the following morning, DeSantis was played back the remarks and gave one of the better retorts you'll ever hear.

"I am working with the president of the United States. I'm working with the director of FEMA," the Federal Emergency Management Agency. "We've been doing this now nonstop for over two weeks," DeSantis told *Fox & Friends*.

Even though Kamala had been veep for three and a half years, DeSantis claimed she had never called him during previous disasters. "Although I've worked well with the president, she has never called Florida. She has never offered any support," he continued. "I don't have time for those games. I don't care about her campaign. Obviously, I'm not a supporter of hers, but she has no role in this process. And so, I'm working with the people I need to be working with."

Boom.

Here's where things got very interesting. *On the very same day* that Kamala bizarrely attacked DeSantis for being selfish, Biden showed he had the governor's back by completely contradicting his own vice president's characterization of the Floridian governor's attitude after a reporter asked about Kamala's allegation against him.

"All I can tell you is I've talked to Governor DeSantis," Biden answered. "He's been very gracious. He thanked me for all we've done. He knows what we're doing, and I think that's important.

"The governor of Florida has been cooperative. He said he's gotten all that he needs. I talked to him again yesterday, and I said—no—you're doing a great job, it's all being done well, and we thank you for it," the president added, while noting that he gave DeSantis his "direct number" if he needed anything.

What a politically devastating moment for the Kamala campaign. And what was truly delicious about the whole thing was that Biden, at that moment, de-aged his brain ten years to sound like 2014 Biden. He was sharp. His voice was strong. He was resolute . . . almost as if he was on a final mission.

"Holy crap, Joe Biden just said Ron DeSantis has his direct number, is doing a great job on hurricane response, directly undercutting Kamala. Biden hates her. Not hiding it now," my friend Clay Travis noted on X. He wasn't wrong.

This last example may not have been intentional on Biden's part, but it sure was damaging to Kamala nonetheless.

The date was October 30, 2024. Seven days to the election. Donald Trump had just held that massive rally at Madison Square Garden when, as we talked about earlier, a comedian made an off-color joke about Puerto Rico's garbage problem. So of course a reporter asked Biden about it, and here's what he said: "The only garbage I see floating out there is his supporters."

Oh boy. It was Hillary's "basket of deplorables" moment all over again and came at the worst possible time for the Kamala campaign, just as it was making its closing argument. Social media absolutely exploded, with Biden's comments going viral to the tune of tens of millions of views, while even legacy media had begrudgingly been forced to cover it.

Trump's response was pitch-perfect after being told about Biden's comment by Marco Rubio at a Trump rally in Pennsylvania.

"Wow. That's terrible," he said while noting Hillary's deplorables comment. "And then she said irredeemable. That didn't work out."

"Garbage, I think, is worse," Trump added. "But [Biden] doesn't know. You have to please forgive him."

Trump wasn't done there either. He saw how successful his Mc-Donald's stop was in Pennsylvania a few weeks earlier and felt he had to continue to troll Kamala and Joe over the garbage comment. And in another masterstroke, the campaign was able to acquire a garbage truck in Green Bay, Wisconsin, which was driven to Green Bay–Austin Straubel International Airport to meet Trump's plane on the tarmac.

"How do you like my garbage truck?" Trump asked reporters from the passenger side while donning an orange and yellow safety vest over a white dress shirt and customary red tie. "This is in honor of Kamala and Joe Biden."

The insufferable Seth Meyers later called the moment "embarrassing" and "surreal" on his late-night "comedy" show.

The pope of late night, Jimmy Kimmel, reacted this way: "I have to say if there is a single image that we will look back on and say, 'This defines what America was going through in 2024,' I think it would be the Republican nominee for president dancing to the song 'YMCA' in a garbage man costume. That vest will come in handy when he's on the side of the highway picking up trash with the other inmates," he said while making a prayer gesture.

Kimmel would cry onstage a week later after Trump won, but more on that later.

The White House, for their part, attempted to edit the official transcript to make it appear Biden was only talking about comedian Tony Hinchcliffe. But no one bought it. X users played fact-checkers and called the White House out for attempting to insult everyone's collective intelligence.

Biden's remark was not all that surprising given the disdain for the working class we've seen from the Democratic Party in recent years.

It seemingly began with Barack Obama as a presidential candidate in 2008 when he was caught on a hot mic saying that flyover-state voters were "bitter" as they "cling to their guns or religion" when it comes to the topic of illegal immigration.

Hillary Clinton just couldn't help herself when she ran for president either, calling Trump supporters a "basket of deplorables" during public remarks that served as a rallying cry for blue-collar voters in Pennsylvania, Michigan, and Wisconsin in particular. Clinton would go on to lose all three "Blue Wall" states that she thought she had all wrapped up to Trump.

On Election Day, Jill Biden went out to cast her vote wearing a bright pantsuit. She could have worn *any* color (except one) that day and we wouldn't have heard a peep about it.

She chose red.

MAGA red.

A few weeks later at the Kennedy Center Honors, Jill took her seat by blowing past Kamala without so much as a glance in her direction. The *New York Post* reported: "Lame duck President Biden and first lady Jill Biden ignored a beaming Vice President Kamala Harris—who was applauding enthusiastically for the couple—as they entered the Kennedy Center Honors to a standing ovation, awkward video shows. The Bidens didn't greet or acknowledge Harris as they entered the 47th Kennedy Center Honors, even as they took a spot standing right next to the vice president her husband, second gentleman Doug Emhoff."

After Trump's victory, Biden graciously invited Trump to the White House. And I swear, and I certainly wasn't alone on this one, I don't think I've ever seen Biden smile so brightly when the two men posed for photographers.

"Look at his fucking smile, dude! That's like when your kid gets married! He lost! His party lost! He was happy!" noted Joe Rogan at the time.

Maybe we'll hear years from now that Jill and Joe Biden voted for Trump. And if we do, ask yourself this question: Given the way they were treated, could you really blame them?

Speaking of Election Day, it had finally come. And this time around, unlike 2020, we would know who won before the sun rose the next day.

Election Night

Number one: Trump's gonna lose. He's gonna lose badly. He's gonna be wrecked. I don't know what the Electoral College count's gonna be at the end of this, but it's gonna get loud and it's gonna get hard for him. Their panic is extraordinary. . . . This is a campaign in free fall.

—RICK WILSON, LINCOLN PROJECT

The day had finally come: Donald John Trump, who had been running for president for a third time for 720 days since announcing his candidacy shortly after the 2022 midterms, was on the verge of doing what no president had done since Grover Cleveland back in the late nineteenth century: win back the White House in nonconsecutive terms.

Election Day itself can be quite boring. No results are revealed until after 7 p.m. eastern time, and no key swing-state results come in until nearly midnight. A terrible precedent had been set by the 2020 election, which took forever to reveal a result, thanks to Democrat policies. The nation held its breath for a repeat. More than a few pundits said it might take at least until the weekend before we would know who won, which is profoundly horrible considering that fewer and fewer voters trust our elections and the process. The more time that goes by after the polls close, the more collective suspicion and anger rises.

Look at 2020. According to the FiveThirtyEight, on November 4, 2020, one day after the election, "Two more batches of [the] Pennsylvania vote were reported: 23,277 votes in Philadelphia, all for Biden."

How is that mathematically possible with three candidates on the ballot? Just asking questions here, kids. Now, sure, we later found out that election officials do sometimes enter votes for one candidate at a time, which is why there was a large chunk of Trump votes in the next update. But why set up a situation where people are waiting and questioning for so long that even the most normal things look suspicious?

In India, their election results are known one day after precincts close. We're talking *640 million ballots*. In Argentina, 99.9 percent of their ballots, more than 27 million, are counted in the span of a few hours. In the United States of America in 2024, we were still counting ballots in states like California *three weeks* after Election Day. It's an absolute joke and reeks of corruption. Then again, this is the home of Gavin Newsom, Nancy Pelosi, Adam Schiff, and Eric Swalwell, so are we remotely surprised?

This book truly does write itself, doesn't it?

The forecasters were also coming in with their final predictions, with nearly all saying Kamala was going to win the popular vote and electoral college: Nate Silver, the *Economist*, FiveThirtyEight, and Larry Sabato's Crystal Ball all gave her the edge despite existing data showing Trump far exceeding expectations in early vote totals.

Ah, Sabato. Mike Lindell's doppelganger. He had Hillary winning 347 electoral votes in 2016 (he was only off by 121). This time around, after ranting about Trump for years while presenting himself as an objective pollster, he clocked in with his final "Crystal Ball" to show Kamala winning 276 electoral votes and therefore the whole race. Garage-sale Magic 8 Balls are more accurate than this guy.

Here's the big data point that stood out to me on Election Day and defied all these predictions: what was happening in Pennsylvania. Kamala held a 400,000-vote lead going into the election in early and mail-in voting. Pretty big lead, right?

Nope. Joe Biden held a 1.1-million-vote lead going into Election Day 2020. He ended up winning the state by 80,000 votes. So if Kamala was 700,000 votes shy of Biden's margin in early voting, how, mathematically, could she win the state?

Then there was the Scott Pressler factor. You've seen Pressler on X by now. He looks like a peripheral character in a Kevin Smith movie, like *Mallrats* or *Clerks*. Long hair, midthirties, has nearly 2 million followers on X, founder of "Gays for Trump."

And as we all witnessed for years, this guy never sleeps. He and his team created a huge ground game in the Keystone State and was able to register thousands of Amish voters alone, most of whom went to Trump. Pressler was such a huge factor that Trump even invited him to speak at a huge rally shortly before the election.

"While Democrats still are the largest party in number in Pennsylvania, the Democratic Party's 286,291 lead in voter registrations—down from 1.2 million at the height of Barack Obama fever in 2008—is now smaller than it's been at any time since 1970," reported Pennsylvania news outlet Lehigh Valley Live in November shortly before the election.

Democrats can't win presidential elections without Pennsylvania; it's that simple. Florida and Ohio are long gone. The blue candidate's path now relies on sweeping the Blue Wall, which has been swept by Trump in two of the last three elections.

Pressler, who set up camp in Pennsylvania in 2021 with the sole focus of registering low-propensity voters, including frat guys at various campuses who ultimately broke for Trump, will now move to New Jersey to attempt to flip the state red. He may very well succeed there too. Pressler explained to *Fox & Friends* after the election that Biden won by 80,000 votes in Pennsylvania, and the state was flipped four years later thanks primarily to getting more rural voters to the polls. He noted that New Jersey went to Kamala by 80,000 in 2024, so why can't this state be flipped by 2028, too? Being a Jersey guy myself, I can safely report that the Garden State is trending red in a big way. In my town of Wyckoff, for example, Trump won by 1 point in 2020. In 2024, he won my town by *17 points*.

I settled in to watch TV coverage in my Fortress of Solitude downstairs. In the Concha house, my wife runs most of the show. She has jurisdiction over every room in terms of style except one: the basement. And being in three fantasy leagues and a bunch of pools during the NFL season, which runs from early September to mid-February, I refuse to ever watch one game or even one commercial, hence this arrangement. It's crude and belongs in my old fraternity house, sure, but maturity was never my strong suit.

MSNBC always has some gems to offer up on big political days, and this one was no exception. "Presidential historian" Michael Beschloss actually made this argument when previewing a possible Trump presidency on *Morning Joe*.

> If historians in the future are allowed to write books, and by the way, that question is open this morning, and if people are allowed to go on television and say what they think in the future, which again, that question is open this morning, in the future, historians are going to look back on this day and say this is the day that America made a choice between freedom and democracy on one side and authoritarianism and dictatorship on the other.

Beschloss sounded like he was auditioning for a *West Wing* remake. "You have to give Donald Trump credit for this," he continued. "He's been very straightforward. He has said, if you elect me, you're going to get violence, you're going to get dictatorship. Or at least today, he has made it very clear what's going to happen. That's a campaign promise. And what I cannot understand is that half the country seems to think that that's fine."

This is such utter garbage. Trump joked about being a dictator on day one in terms of executive orders to secure the border and drill, baby, drill. Clowns like Beschloss know exactly what Trump's context was and say this crap anyway in an effort to instill fear in the audience. He sells cheap hyperbole, like Trump banning historians from writing books in the future or banning opinions on channels like MSNBC, and gets away with it because there are no adults with any spine running that place.

On Fox News, we're never told what to say. Ever. But if I ever made such reckless statements as Beschloss did, I'm certain I'd be called into an important person's office somewhere at headquarters and asked to present proof behind my claims. And if I couldn't back it up, there would be accountability. That's why I prepare the way I do for every appearance: because I never want to have that conversation.

Meanwhile, over on CNN in the afternoon, political "analyst" Nia-Malika Henderson had this to say about the way the two candidates closed as she was living on another planet.

"They closed in very different ways. Kamala Harris closed with an upbeat vision, and you had Donald Trump all about grievance and sort of talking down to Americans, being racist and sexist," she said while wearing the largest eyeglasses not seen on a human being since Clark Kent. By the way, Kamala's closing argument was literally calling Trump a fascist. That didn't seem . . . upbeat.

That evening, after Florida was quickly called for Trump, who ended up winning by 13 points, Joy Reid went to ludicrous speed in a hurry.

"It's a pure Project 2025 in miniature in Florida," Reid ranted. "That kind of extremist right-wing, fascist-type government in Florida—does that make it a more attractive place—or does it make it more like some of the other southern states that don't get investment?"

Nothing further, Your Honor.

The evening's first exit polls appeared to show Trump running ahead of expectations and Kamala struggling in key urban areas like Philadelphia, Charlotte, and Atlanta. This prompted panic from PBS's Jonathan Capehart, who hilariously went with this hot mess of a take:

"I am mystified that Trump is gaining support from 2020. The twice-impeached, four-times-indicted, convicted of 34 felony counts . . . ? After Madison Square Garden!? Who are we as a country? . . . I'm not sure I like it!"

Yep. This was the same guy we mentioned earlier in the book who really thought Trump's Madison Square Garden rally was an ode to Nazism. Of course he was surprised.

Back over on CNN, Jake Tapper seemed shocked when asking resident map guy John King regarding where Kamala may have been gaining on Biden's 2020 performance.

"You asked: 'Are there any places that the vice president is over-performing Joe Biden in 2020?'" King repeated back before showing a completely dark map indicating Kamala didn't gain . . . *anywhere*.

"Holy smokes," Tapper said in response. "Literally nothing?"

"Literally nothing," King reiterated.

"Literally not *one* county?" Tapper asked again.

"There might be more out here on the West Coast," King replied unconvincingly.

At this point, I had joined Pete Hegseth for our *Fox Nation* special covering election results as they came in. It was truly a career highlight, having never covered an Election Night live before and analyzing the results as they came in. And I was seeing the same things John King and Bill Hemmer over on Fox News were seeing: Kamala wasn't going to get there.

In fact, my prediction of winning every swing state was looking better and better: Trump was outperforming in the suburbs and rural areas, while Kamala was underperforming in the cities. States like New Hampshire and New Jersey had much tighter margins coming in, with Trump gaining significantly in both, barely losing the Granite State while only losing by 5 in New Jersey (Biden had won in Jersey by 16 in 2020, therefore showing an 11-point swing to Trump). She got blown out in Florida, Ohio, and, of course, Iowa. There wasn't one red state

Kamala was going to come close to flipping, but there were six Trump could flip from the 2020 election.

North Carolina was the first swing state to be called, at 11:18 p.m. eastern. Georgia was next, at 12:58 a.m., as there were no pipes that decided to burst this time around. Kamala's only hope was to win Pennsylvania, Michigan, and Wisconsin, and that wasn't magically going to happen, given what we saw in the Southeast.

By that time, I was seeing almost no path for Harris, while Republicans were picking off Senate seats in Montana, Ohio, and West Virginia while still neck-and-neck in Wisconsin, Michigan, and Pennsylvania. There wasn't one positive data point for Kamala, with her path becoming nearly impossible. And her campaign had gone stone silent.

Ninety minutes later, as the clock approached midnight, King called the race for Trump on CNN, declaring: "He's going to get there. I'm probably not supposed to say that on television. But he's going to get there."

At 1:46 a.m., Fox News called the race for Trump after Wisconsin was put in his column.

"The former president's comeback will be complete with a win in Wisconsin, a state that he narrowly lost four years ago," reported Martha MacCallum out of Fox's cavernous Studio M in New York. "He is now the second president in U.S. history to win nonconsecutive terms. The first was Grover Cleveland in the late 1800s. Senator JD Vance will become the fiftieth vice president of the United States."

Trump would go on to capture 312 electoral votes. He flipped six states Biden had won in 2020: Pennsylvania, Michigan, Wisconsin, Arizona, Nevada, and Georgia. Some more fun numbers: Hillary won Beverly Hills by 31 points in 2016, Trump won it by 5 points in 2024. Hillary won Starr County, Texas, a border town, by 60 points in 2016, Trump won it by 16 in 2024 (a 76-point flip). Trump won married men by 22 points, married women by 3. He also won among unmarried men. Kamala won among only unmarried women.

Overall, if looking at a satellite map and filling in the votes, 86.72 percent of the country is red, while 13.28 percent of the country is blue.

In the end, the early vote totals had held. Trump's decision to push early voting after not embracing it in 2020 proved to be the right one.

Trump took to the stage live at a rally in Palm Beach at 2:27 a.m. to declare victory, which was almost the exact same time the race was called for him in 2016.

Trump, dressed in his standard navy suit and MAGA red tie, looked and sounded like a commanding general thanking his troops after conquering the enemy.

> This is the greatest political movement of all time. There's never been anything like this in this country. I want to thank the American people for the extraordinary honor of being elected your forty-seventh president—and your forty-fifth president.
>
> And to every citizen, I will fight for you, for your family, and your future. Every single day I will be fighting for you, and with every breath in my body. I will not rest until we have delivered the strong, safe, and prosperous America that our children deserve and that you deserve. This will truly be the golden age of America. That's what we have to have. This is a magnificent victory for the American people that will allow us to make America great again.

Politicians like to throw that line out all the time: they'll fight for you. But with Trump, when he says "Fight! Fight! Fight!" after being shot or impeached or put on one trial after another or compared to Hitler over and over again, you know he truly means it.

There was also this campaign slogan that really resonated while simultaneously trolling: "Kamala Harris is for they/them, Donald Trump is for you."

That's one for the ages.

It was an extraordinary moment that put everything into context. This man had every powerful entity aimed at him: the Justice Department, the FBI, two presidential administrations, the media, and two assassins, yet he *still* won bigly. This truly was the greatest comeback of all time. The ultimate American story of perseverance and redemption. And he did it all at seventy-eight years old.

The most delicious chapter of this book is coming up: the reactions, the meltdowns, the ramifications, and a future full of optimism. November 2024, from start to finish, was one hell of a ride.

Take a seat, grab some popcorn, and enjoy the implosions.

The Delicious Aftermath

Just twenty-four hours after Kamala Harris was defeated, the rhetorical swords were out for Joe Biden.

It was delightful, yet sad, to watch.

Poor Joe. The worst president of our lifetime went from Dems saying he should be on (checks notes) Mount Rushmore to being the end result of an unsuccessful coup waged against him by his own party (namely Nancy Pelosi and Barack Obama), who proceeded to offer up the worst presidential candidate in U.S. history in Kamala.

I'm not kidding about the Biden-on-Mount-Rushmore-thing either: It reminds me of a great scene from *Seinfeld* after the hapless George Costanza gets hired by the New York Yankees when he insults George Steinbrenner to his face. In the 1994 episode, George is convinced by Jerry to ignore every instinct he's ever had and do the opposite in *every* situation. So upon interviewing to join the Yankees back office, he meets the team's then-bombastic (and iconic) owner.

Steinbrenner: *Nice to meet you (extends his hand for a handshake, but George ignores it and jumps right in with his true feelings on how Steinbrenner had run the team to that point, which was the opposite of what George normally would have done here).*

George: *Well, I wish I could say the same, but I must say, with all due respect, I find it very hard to see the logic behind some of the moves you have made with this fine organization. In the past twenty years you have caused myself, and the city of New*

York, a good deal of distress, as we have watched you take our beloved Yankees and reduced them to a laughing stock, all for the glorification of your massive ego!

Steinbrenner *(no pause)*: *Hire this man!*

Constanza responds with an incredulous look that the opposite actually worked. So after he's hired for his dream job, he runs to Jerry's apartment to share the news that he was actually hired.

Jerry *(incredulous)*: *"Ruth, Gehrig, DiMaggio, Mantle . . . COSTANZA?!"*

So when we hear that Democrats like Nancy Pelosi were actually touting Biden as worthy of being on Mount Rushmore, it evokes the same reaction. "Washington, Jefferson, Lincoln, Roosevelt . . . Biden?!"

Yes, the guy who gave us the worst inflation in forty years, massive debt, rampant crime, a lawless border, two wars, and zero confidence in his ability to govern because he was on a Delaware beach for perpetually long weekends for four years as his brain turned to mush . . . *He* deserved to be considered alongside Washington, Jefferson, Abe, and Teddy?

Come on, man!

Everything changed after Biden's debate disaster in Atlanta. So Pelosi, showing who really runs the show, stepped in to save the day.

"The campaign, I thought, was not going in the right direction, and I expressed my concern about that," Pelosi shared in an interview before the election. "I think his legacy had to be protected. I didn't see that happening in the course that it was on, the election was on."

Isn't that nice? A major party decides just three months before an election that its candidate is going to lose, so they simply replace him without any say from even one voter. And yes, Pelosi actually said this once in an interview with CBS News in early 2024.

Biden is "such a consequential president of the United States, a Mount Rushmore kind of president," she said at the time. "You have Teddy Roosevelt up there. And he's wonderful. I don't say take him down. But you can add Biden."

Like Kamala, Nancy Pelosi is a media creation. She represents San Francisco, yet has only helped to destroy a great city once considered the crown jewel of the country. No city has seen a bigger exodus out of it than the City by the Bay in recent years, according to U-Haul. And quality of life has plummeted due to rampant crime due to soft/nonexistent crime laws leading to that exodus.

So when looking back on how the Democratic Party lost the White House because it tried to game the system Soviet-style by usurping the democratic process (all in the name of "saving democracy," ironically), don't blame Kamala as much as Pelosi, who quarterbacked this coup thinking she was smarter than everyone else. Again. This massive loss, from which the party may not recover from for decades, along with her childish act of tearing up the Trump State of the Union speech in 2020, will be what she's remembered for most.

Our stupid media, of course, meanwhile, didn't learn a thing from Trump's massive victory. They live in an elite bubble that only sees people through racial and gender or sexual orientation prisms. And boy, we got a ton of that kind of garbage rhetoric thrown at us after Trump was declared the victor in the early morning hours of November 6.

"If you're brown, you may not stick around," Joyless Reid declared on MSNBC. "I don't think they care whether you have a green card or not. They're pulling people out and taking people out of this country, whether they like it or not or whether you voted for them or not."

Yep. A prime-time host on a "news" network just said without ambiguity that regardless of whether you're a legal citizen or not, under Trump 2.0 you may be deported out of the country simply based on your skin color . . . that American citizens are going to be pulled out of their homes and thrown out. Because that's what totally happened during Trump's first term (sarc).

Joy would go on to delete her X account after the election, claiming she was the victim of "abuse."

MSNBC, just three weeks after the election, saw its lowest ratings in twenty years, averaging just 38,000 viewers in the key 25–54 demo that advertisers base their commercial buys on. Think about that: The network is in more than ninety million homes and can only get 38,000 people in a huge age demographic to watch.

And those viewers, given all the choices out there in the podcast and social media worlds, ain't coming back. How about CNN's Van Jones? I actually think Van is a reasonable guy and gives honest analysis when he doesn't allow his emotions to get to him.

On the night of the election, after it was called for Trump, he allowed just that.

"I'm thinking about the people who are not a part of anybody's elite who are hurting tonight," said Jones as his eyes welled up. "There are African American women who know a little bit about being talked down to, and know a little bit about having their economic dreams crushed, who tried to dream a big dream over the past couple of months. And tonight, they're trading in a lot of hope for a lot of hurt."

He's right about one thing: African American women do know about having their economic dreams crushed under Joe Biden and Kamala Harris. Grocery prices were up on average nearly 25 percent, gas prices were up nearly 50 percent, car insurance was up more than 50 percent, and national home prices rose 45 percent, while nearly half of U.S. renters spend nearly *one-third* of their income on housing, according to CNN.

But in Van's eyes, in this case, African Americans were going to ignore all of this impacting them and cast a vote based solely on race and gender. He makes nice money over at CNN, so the cost of everyday items like food isn't a problem for him. And that's the whole problem with so many on TV: they can't relate to their viewers given their income, their status, and their lack of exposure to the real world.

How about Sunny Hostin, who is considered part of the ABC News division as a cohost of *The View*? "I worry about my children's future, especially my daughter, who now has less rights than I have," she said with her voice quaking the day after Trump won. "I remember my father telling me many, many years ago that I was the first person in his family to enjoy full civil rights. And now I have less civil rights than I had when he told me that."

What the hell is she talking about? What rights have been taken away for her daughter? Abortion? Because Sunny's daughter lives in New York, and abortion will be available in that state in perpetuity, as it is in most other states in the country. Besides, Trump is firmly against a national abortion ban, and any Republican who even proposes refederalizing the abortion issue 1) would be committing political suicide and 2) wouldn't be able to overturn the Supreme Court *Dobbs* decision anyway.

Sunny also managed to play the elitist card in slamming white female Trump voters who don't have a college degree like she does. "Black women tried to save this country again, last night," she said. "What we do not have is white women, who voted about 52 percent for Donald Trump, [who are] uneducated white women is my understanding."

In a related story, just 37 percent of the country overall have earned four-year college degrees. So there's nothing like a pompous millionaire like Sunny insulting a good chunk of her "uneducated" viewers to make a clueless point.

Okay, maybe David Axelrod can bring some common sense to the table. "Let's be honest about this. Let's be absolutely blunt about it: There were appeals to racism in this campaign, and there is racial bias in this country, and there is sexism in this country," Axelrod argued on CNN.

Okay, maybe not. Let's unpack this: Kamala Harris, who was rejected by *Democratic voters* in the 2019 primaries, is the victim of racism and sexism, David? That's a hell of a way to talk about the party base. And if there's so much sexism in this country, how did Hillary Clinton win the popular vote in 2016 again?

How about MSNBC's Joe Scarborough, the former Republican congressman who interviewed Trump *forty-one times* on his morning show in the friendliest of ways leading up to the 2016 election.

"Democrats need to be mature, and they need to be honest. And they need to say, 'Yes, there is misogyny, but it's not just misogyny from white men,'" the former Republican opined on November 6.

"It's misogyny from Hispanic men, it's misogyny from black men—things we've all been talking about—who do not want a woman leading them," Scarborough said while arguing that if Kamala was a six-foot-four man from Arkansas or Florida, she probably would have won.

No . . . she still would have lost.

Say it with me, Joe:

Inflation.

Crime.

Border.

Wars.

Woke/identity politics, censorship.

Weaponization of the government against political opponents.

Blatant dishonesty.

That's why Kamala and the Dems lost.

And again, here's another rich white person lecturing minorities on what is and what isn't racist. In another related story, *Morning Joe* has four primary hosts: Joe, Mika, Willie Geist, and Jonathan Lemire. You'll never guess which skin color they all have in common.

To sum up the meltdowns, here's the Top 10 for the rest of November.

10. Stephen Colbert (sad face): "The majority has spoken and they said they don't care that much about democracy. And I want to take a moment to congratulate Kamala Harris & Tim Walz on running an amazing 107-day campaign."

196 THE GREATEST COMEBACK EVER

This is the same guy who said he didn't mind paying twice as much for gas because he owns an electric car, and therefore you should vote for Democrats to save democracy because, you know, who can't afford an electric car?!

9. Former (losing) Democratic senatorial candidate Rick Taylor on X: "My aunt called asking about Thanksgiving plans. During the conversation she mentioned she voted for Trump. I told her my home is not open to traitors and I would not go to theirs. I have no space in my life for those who could care less about the United States. She's upset."

How this guy didn't get elected is simply incredible.

8. (An especially peeved) James Carville's message to Democrats running campaigns like Kamala's: "We have no legislative power, we have no executive power, we have no judicial power. . . . What you've done ain't worth a shit. Get your head around that. And all of the Washington-based Democrats farting around, going to wine and cheese parties, and talking about how misogynistic the race is, get your ass out of Washington, and go work on a 2026 campaign and do penance to make up for your goddamn arrogance and stupidity.

"Well, we're going to say we told you so. We told you this identity shit was a disaster. We told you to get out in front of public safety issues. You didn't. We told you to have an open process and demonstrate the magnificent and staggering and deep talent that exists in the modern Democratic Party. You didn't. We told you to differentiate yourself from Biden. You didn't. I hate to be some fucking know-it-all, but all of these things are part of the record."

Amen.

7. Katie Couric, who couldn't have been more sycophantic if she tried during a fawning interview with Kamala a few months earlier when she didn't challenge her even once, had this to say after the election on her inability to answer questions in a clear, straightforward manner: "You know, people notice that, and it's like, 'Answer the goddamn question, please!'"

Katie made this comment during her little-known podcast from her kitchen, by the way.

6. Jimmy Kimmel (while crying on the air): "It was a terrible night for women, for children, for the hundreds of thousands of hardworking immigrants who make this country go, for health care, for our climate, for science, for journalism, for justice, for free speech. It was a terrible night for poor people, for the middle class, for seniors who rely on Social Security, for our allies in Ukraine, for NATO, for the truth and democracy and decency. It was a terrible night for everyone who voted against him. And guess what? It was a bad night for everyone who voted for him too. You just don't realize it yet."

Oh, I can watch this again and again. And I have . . .

5. Claire McCaskill (while sobbing on MSNBC). "I'm so proud of her. I don't think people realize how hard it is to get to where she was."

Ummm . . . she was handed the vice presidency in 2020 without receiving one vote. She was handed the nomination in 2024 without receiving one vote. How precisely was it hard to get to where she was?

4. Director Adam McKay of *Anchorman* and anti-Trump fame: "Who would have guessed lying about Biden's cognitive

health for two years, refusing to do an open convention for a new nominee, never mentioning public healthcare & embracing fracking, the Cheneys and a yearlong-slaughter of children in Gaza wouldn't be a winning strategy? Anyone with half a brain?"

McKay announced two days after the election that he was leaving the Democratic Party for good.

3. The *Washington Post*'s onetime "conservative" columnist Jennifer Rubin: "It is 1933. Hitler is in power. No time for a fucking seminar on Democrats' messaging errors."

Also Rubin: "You have to boil it down to nuts and bolts and you have to be pithy. What do I mean by pithy? How about this: Republicans want to kill your kids. It's actually true."

Rubin decided to put her X account into protective mode after Trump's victory, which means preventing anyone from seeing her posts unless they are an "approved follower" of hers. That's courage in your convictions, right there.

2. #NeverTrump Bill Kristol of *The Bulwark*: "The markets are underestimating how radical Trump can be, how much he wants to show that he has personal power, and he wants to remove any sources of opposition certainly in Congress and the Senate."

In the span of one month after Trump's win, the Dow Jones Industrial Average was up more than 2,500 points on optimism that a second Trump term would bring lower inflation, higher wages, less regulation, enhanced GDP growth, and domestic energy production, along with greatly reduced government spending. To Bill Kristol, Dan Quayle's former chief of staff, that's *radical*.

1. Joe Scarborough and Mika Brzezinski: "For those asking why we would speak to the president-elect during such fraught times, I would ask back: Why wouldn't we?" Brzezinski asked her viewers just six days after the election to meet with Trump at Mar-a-Lago to "reset the relationship."

"It's time to do something different, and that starts with not only talking about Donald Trump, but talking with him."

As I said in reaction on Fox News at the time, Joe and Mika are the two phoniest people in the business. It ain't even close. These are two people who only want *access to power* just so they can brag to their viewers and friends about having such access.

They craved that power in 2015–16 when Trump first ran for office. They moved over to Biden in 2020. Stories were leaked out of the Biden White House about how *Morning Joe* was his favorite show (if you believe Biden was even awake in the early morning). Scarborough would brag about speaking to Biden and those close to him for most of the four years of his presidency as some kind of invaluable insider. Now, with Trump back in power, there they were at Mar-a-Lago in *under a week* to kiss the ring.

To Trump's immense credit, he was magnanimous in accepting the meeting. He could have told them to go fuck off for comparing him to Hitler and accusing him of planning to destroy the Constitution and execute his opponents. But why punch down when you can have two of your biggest, most narcissistic critics crawl to your estate and beg for forgiveness? Sounds fun.

"I received a call from Joe Scarborough requesting a meeting for him and Mika, and I agreed that it would be a good thing if such meeting took place," Trump told Brooke Singman of FoxNews.com that day. "We met at Mar-a-Lago on Friday morning at 8:00.

"Many things were discussed, and I very much appreciated the fact that they wanted to have open communication. In many ways, it's too bad that it wasn't done long ago," added Trump.

Also note: Trump is a master troll. And what better way to drive the likes of Rachel Maddow and Nicolle Wallace and Joy Reid into an absolute tizzy than doing a friendly interview on *their network*? Nonetheless, Megyn Kelly had the perfect reaction to Joe and Mika's patent hypocrisy on her SiriusXM podcast. "I searched for a way to respond appropriately, and I called on my ten years as a litigator, in addition to my now twenty as a journalist, and I think I found the perfect phrase: Go fuck yourselves. Go fuck yourselves. Go fuck yourselves. You dishonest jokes of faux journalists. What an absurd farce . . . Which one was insincere? He's Hitler? Or now we're going to speak truth to power and find a way of speaking to and working with Donald Trump? Which one was a lie?!"

Listen to Megyn's podcast if you haven't. *It's that good.* The cope extended to the basketball world as well, with Golden State Warriors head coach Steve Kerr announcing that he was so distraught due to Trump's victory, he didn't have the fortitude to coach the Warriors' game against the defending champion Boston Celtics the day after the election.

"I don't know if I'm capable of coaching basketball knowing Donald Trump is our president," an emotional Kerr told reporters. "I certainly won't be on the sidelines tonight. I need some time to digest this tragedy for our country."

If I were Golden State's owner, I'd have suspended him without pay or considered an outright firing for this. Do your job and grow a pair, Steve. Oh, and without Michael Jordan or Steph Curry, you don't have one championship to your name. Just sayin' . . .

You also didn't say jack when the NBA raked in boatloads of money from the Chinese government despite their human rights abuses and outright internment camps of the Uigurs, so your words here are just a bit hollow. Just resign and go work for Gavin Newsom's 2028 campaign as his spokesman already.

Outspoken liberal Cenk Uygur also weighed in during an interview with Representative Steve Cohen (D-TN). At least he seemed to get that insulting Trump supporters is not a good idea.

"So what does that make the Democratic Party if you lose to [Trump] twice?" Cenk asked.

Cohen replied: "It may be the American electorate. Some of them are selfish and greedy. They want lower tax rates, to give more money to their kids in the lucky sperm club. . . . A lot of whites thought blacks are getting handouts. . . . If you give up all the money, you're not helping yourself."

"I think blaming the American electorate is a bad idea," Uygur correctly replied.

As for AOC, she removed her pronouns from her bio on X. A total surrender.

Bill Maher had plenty to say after the election, and as usual when it comes to the woke nonsense inside his own party, he hit the bull's-eye.

> You wear "Queers for Palestine" T-shirts and masks two years after the pandemic ended. And you can't define a woman. I mean "person who menstruates." You're the teachers' union education party and you've turned schools and colleges into a joke. You just lost a crazy contest to an actual crazy person.
>
> Democrats have become like a royal family that, because of so much incest, has unfortunately had children who are retarded. And the same thing can happen to ideas if they are also conceived in an atmosphere of intellectual incest. Maybe take the clothespins off your noses and actually converse with the other half of the country. Stop screaming at people to get with the program and instead make a program worth getting with.

Bravo.

Senator John Fetterman also showed real balls. Again. Here's what he had to say about Nancy Pelosi, who was once deemed untouchable.

"She's the godmother, she's the enforcer. And now she's blaming Biden. Well, you can't have it both ways. You got what you wanted, and now you're still blaming Biden. I think it's really ironic that you have a woman at age eighty-four and she is still hanging on. Why not give a younger generation an opportunity to occupy that seat?"

This version of Fetterman is *really* likable.

The *New York Times* and Frank Luntz interviewed undecided voters after election day. Here were their reasons for voting the way they did. And it's (can't stop using this word) delicious.

> *I voted Trump. I made the decision after he appeared on Joe Rogan. He just seemed more normal than the other side.*
>
> —JOSEPH, TWENTY-FOUR, VOTED FOR BIDEN IN 2020.

> *I voted for Donald Trump. I decided after Kamala went on Call Her Daddy.–*
>
> —PIERCE, TWENTY-SIX, NORTH CAROLINA, WHITE,
> SALES, DIDN'T VOTE IN 2020

> *I shocked myself and voted for Trump. No one tell my family. I was so impressed by JD Vance, the way he carried himself and how normal he appeared. I think I became radicalized on the men and women's sports issue. The ad that said, "Kamala represents they/them. Trump represents you," that was so compelling.*
>
> —MCLANE, TWENTY-FIVE, D.C., WHITE,
> LEGAL FIELD, WROTE IN ROMNEY IN 2020

> *The Joe Rogan interview was huge for me. Trump enthusiastically said yes to a three-hour, open, honest conversation with Joe Rogan, who was a former Bernie bro. I think it's very telling about which candidate is authentic and which candidate is not.*
>
> —JACK, TWENTY-TWO, NEW YORK, WHITE,
> UNDERWRITER, VOTED BIDEN IN 2020

Over on X, an account called "Trump Is My President" kept an active log of celebrities and lawmakers who vowed to leave the country if elected . . . so say bye-bye to these fine folks! If they keep their word, anyway (most won't): Alec Baldwin, Whoopi Goldberg, John Legend, Chrissy Teigen, Rob Reiner, Barbara Streisand, Cher, Nancy Pelosi, Hillary Clinton, Megan Rapinoe, Tom Hanks, Amy Schumer, AOC, Lady Gaga, Taylor Swift, Bill Gates, Jane Fonda, Madonna, Mark Ruffalo, Kim Kardashian, Bruce Springsteen, George Clooney, Hunter Biden, Oprah Winfrey, Robert De Niro, Samuel L. Jackson, Miley Cyrus, Travis Kelce, Bobbi Althoff, Rashida Tlaib, Stormy Daniels, Dr. Anthony Fauci, George Soros, Diddy (who would have to escape from jail), Eminem, Ellen DeGeneres, Sean Penn, Sharon Stone, Ashley Judd, Tommy Lee, Bryan Cranston, Billie Joe Armstrong (Green Day's lead singer).

Cher also promised to blow her brains out while meathead Rob Reiner said he'd set himself on fire. Totally normal. But give Ellen DeGeneres some credit, I guess. She actually moved to London after the election.

"I think, unfortunately, the Democratic Party has the stench of loser written all over the party," Democratic fundraiser Lindy Li told *Fox and Friends Weekend* after the election. "I feel like the Democrats are going to consigned to the wilderness for at least the next four to eight years." She would later announce she was leaving the party after receiving multiple threats from inside the party for simply being honest about the state of the party and appearing on networks like Fox.

Overall, and this sums up our media nicely, according to the Media Research Center, Harris received 78 percent positive coverage to Trump's 15 percent across ABC, NBC, and CBS. Talk about a disconnect with the public considering Trump just won easily.

Speaking of ABC, they decided to settle a $15 million defamation suit leveled against them by Trump in December 2024. Trump rightly sued after George Stephanopoulos, in the span of just one interview with Representative Nancy Mace, falsely stated on ten occasions that Trump had been convicted of rape. He most certainly was not. The network, likely fearing what would come out in discovery through emails and texts (remember, Kamala's best friend runs ABC News), so they wrote a check to Trump's future library, as well as paying for his legal costs. Stephanopoulos reportedly was fuming behind the scenes about the settlement. Good. This is the same guy who ran a smear campaign out of the White House against Bill Clinton's sexual assault accusers back in the nineties, so of course ABC rewarded him with a fat contract and two shows on the network.

One Democrat who always makes more sense than most, regardless of party, is Mark Penn, arguably the most sensible person in polling when it comes to understanding what America is thinking. I worked multiple polling-centric events with Mark during my time at the *Hill* and was always beyond impressed with his interpretation of what the data was telling him.

Here was his take on the morning after the election on X:

It should come as no great surprise that a Democratic Party, which has abandoned working class people, would find that the working class has abandoned them. While the Democratic leadership defends the status quo, the American people are angry and want change. And they're right.

Lessons of the election America is a center right country at heart. Only 25 percent are liberal and the other 75 percent won't be ruled by the 25. Campaigns are about issues and serious proposals and positions and you can't avoid having them. Demonizing opponents and using lawfare to try to jail your opponents can and will backfire.

Voters don't listen to Hollywood celebrities when it comes to voting. Most voters see Hollywood as great for entertaining but as far removed from their concerns when it comes to voting.

The working class and middle America voters are done being disrespected by college elites. They want real, merit-based opportunities, not government subsidies. Identity politics is ultimately losing politics as voters care more about issues not identity when living their lives.

Young people are waking up and beginning to reject woke politics and their turn to the center is the surprise of the election. America wants a country with real borders and a working immigration system. The mainstream media allowed itself to become a tool for a political party and an ideology and needs to reform itself.

So much to unpack here from Penn. For example, Trump flipped young men to his corner by *30 points* from 2020. Among young women, the shift was 17 points, according to Associated Press exit polls. We've been told forever that if young voters come out, Democrats will win. That can't be said anymore.

As for the national media reforming itself, that's never going to happen as long as they exist primarily in New York and Washington, D.C. The clowns run the circus now, and those ecosystems in those deep-blue cities make it ideologically impossible to be truly balanced, especially with Democrat donors running the show at the top.

Exhibit A on this front is what happened at NBC News in the spring of 2024 with the ouster of former RNC chairwoman Ronna McDaniel less than forty-eight hours after she was hired. It marked a disturbing pattern for those who actually care about free speech and the most important diversity of all: diversity of thought.

To review, McDaniel got hired to be a contributor by NBC—and the "talent" immediately and publicly revolted. "The fact that Ms. McDaniel is on the payroll at NBC News, to me that is inexplicable," Rachel Maddow told her viewers. "And I hope they will reverse their decision."

Chuck Todd also weighed in on the air after McDaniel made her one and only appearance on the network before getting canned.

"There's a reason a lot of journalists at NBC News are uncomfortable with this," Todd told Kristen Welker on his former program *Meet the Press*, alleging that McDaniel engaged in "gaslighting" and "character assassination" when dealing with the press.

"I think our bosses owe you an apology for putting you in this situation," Todd also told Welker. The next day, Joe and Mika threatened to walk off the *Morning Joe* set in protest if McDaniel was booked on their show, where she might, God forbid, say something positive about Trump while taking Democrats to task.

Management, instead of telling these petulant adult children to cease criticizing the hire and them publicly, caved quickly instead—and McDaniel was gone.

Just last year, CNN attempted to move to the center by having the audacity under its new network president, Chris Licht, to host Donald Trump—the odds-on favorite to be president again—for a town hall. Note: CNN had hosted Trump multiple times in the same capacity leading up to the 2016 election. But in 2023, on-air talent carried out a full mutiny on the air.

One night after the Trump town hall that was well received by those in attendance, Anderson Cooper actually said this directly to viewers: "You have every right to be outraged today, and angry, and never watch this network again," he said while calling Trump's appearance "disturbing."

A few days later, the inmates won again. Licht was shown the door. Jake Tapper, who fancies himself as a straight and serious anchor, shared that the network was better off for it.

"Our North Star here at CNN has always been the journalism, not preaching to the choir. We are not an entertainment company with a news division. We are a news company," he shared. And he actually believes that.

The same thing happened at *Politico* over tapping Ben Shapiro to edit its *Politico Playbook* for one day a few years back. Staffers took issue and in a very public way. When any other political pundit or host was tapped to do the same thing from the left, not a peep was ever heard. Shapiro was never invited back. See how this works?

November 2024, at least until this moment, was the best time of Donald Trump's life. Not just because of his resounding victory. Not just epic meltdowns that followed. But also because lawfare, as we knew it against him, was dead.

In New York, the so-called hush money case, the one where Trump was found guilty in an environment so rigged against him it's hard to put into words, was supposed to see Trump get sentenced by Judge Juan Merchan in September 2024.

You remember Merchan, the judge whose adult daughter literally had clients who raised $93 million over a period where they were also sending out solicitation emails focusing on the Trump case. Naah . . . no conflict of interest there whatsoever.

"Judge" Merchan would go on to sentence Trump on January 10, 2025, just ten days before Trump took office. The sentence, of course, included zero punishment. Instead, it was simply done so the media could run with the "Trump is the first convicted felon ever to assume the presidency" line. Convicted of what? That still is patently unclear.

After the sentencing was delayed until after the election, Trump's victory compelled Merchan to postpone sentencing until after he leaves office. Given what thin gruel this case was, something no person on the planet has ever served jail time for, it will surely be thrown out on appeal, according to most legal experts.

In Georgia, Fani Willis tanked her own RICO case against Trump by hiring her (married) lawyer boyfriend who might as well have been the nonfictional version of *Better Call Saul* lawyer Saul Goodman. Willis paid Wade $600,000 in taxpayer funds to try the case despite him never having handled a RICO case in his life. The scam was quickly exposed, and the case was all but dead.

In December 2024, a Fulton County judge ordered Willis to hand over all communications to Special Counsel Jack Smith, who was supposed to be running a separate investigation entirely. Why would she be in contact with him?

Unless . . .

Speaking of Jack Smith, he announced in late November 2024 that he was dropping both the federal documents and January 6 cases against Trump in light of his victory, saying he had "no choice" but to do so.

Democrats really screwed themselves on this front. Whether it was legal efforts to take Trump off state ballots, which was temporarily successful in Maine and Colorado before the Supreme Court stepped in, or whether it was the sexual assault case brought forth by E. Jean Carroll decades later when she couldn't even remember what year the alleged assault occurred, or all the aforementioned cases that were clearly politically motivated, the party showed they do not care about democracy or the rule of law.

If they wanted to beat Trump, they should have stuck to concentrating on doing so at the ballot box. Hopefully these failures will cause both parties to think twice about embracing the third world and attempting to win elections in this despicable fashion. Because the public hates it.

Despite all these headwinds, the forty-fifth president became our forty-seventh president-elect around 2:30 a.m. on November 6. But don't expect the insanity to stop until January 2029. Fortunately, no sane or sober person is listening anymore.

One could only imagine just how bad a Kamala-Walz administration would have been. How bad? Just check out the way they blew through more than $1 billion in a matter of three months, only to end up in massive debt.

The Billion-Dollar-Plus Bust

They say money can't buy happiness.

Especially if you're the Kamala Harris campaign . . .

One of the most revealing aspects of the 2024 election was just how inept Kamala's people running the campaign were. Think about it: How does a political operation only exist for three months blow through *one-point-five billion dollars*?

In contrast, the Trump campaign raised $380 million since she was installed and spent only $350 million of it. Compare that to Team Kamala, who was forced to beg for money through fundraising emails *after* the election to cover the $20 million in debt on top of the billion it spent.

Trump, at his best when he has the wind at his back as the happy warrior, like we saw at the Al Smith Dinner and at McDonald's in Pennsylvania or in the back of that garbage truck in Wisconsin, decided to offer Kamala a helping hand.

He's the Don Rickles of presidents in modern next-level trolling terms four days after the election:

> I am very surprised that the Democrats, who fought a hard and valiant fight in the 2020 Presidential Election, raising a record amount of money, didn't have lots of $'s left over. Now they are being squeezed by vendors and others. Whatever we can do to help them during this difficult period, I would strongly recommend we, as a Party and for the sake of desperately needed UNITY, do. We have a lot of money left over in that our biggest

asset in the campaign was "Earned Media," and that doesn't cost very much. MAKE AMERICA GREAT AGAIN!

And really, think about this for a moment: Kamala had easily more than doubled the amount of money she had raised in the homestretch compared to Trump.

And she lost.

She had most of the legacy media on her side.

And she lost.

She had basically all of Hollywood.

And she lost.

Most importantly, she had five times the speaking accents at rallies depending on location and venue.

And she lost. Badly.

It gets worse when you peel the onion off the Harris campaign expenditures; it's absolute insanity drenched in comedy gold.

Remember that Oprah interview Kamala did during her media blitz a few weeks before the election? On the surface, it appeared that the former Queen of all Media and Harris were old friends and Oprah—a staunch Democrat and close with the Obamas—was simply doing her a favor by providing her the journalistic version of a hot stone massage in a fixed town-hall setting where all questions were reviewed and approved.

The "interview" didn't make news, as Kamala's conversations in these settings never do. The real story came after the election, when we learned that the campaign paid Oprah's production company—a billionaire, mind you—$1 million for the effort. Did she need the money? We were told this was an organic, genuine effort by Oprah to save democracy by getting Kamala elected.

Or . . . and I'm just spitballing here: this whole spectacle, like everything else in this cartoon of a campaign, was scripted, manufactured, and phony.

It gets better. According to a Fox News report after the ballots were counted, the campaign also shelled out six figures to build a studio set for Kamala's interview with Alex Cooper of the *Call Her Daddy* podcast. What . . . the existing set wasn't good enough?

"The Harris campaign spent, like, $100,000," explained Cooper in an interview with CNBC's Adam Ross Sorkin after the election. "My studio that is gorgeous in Los Angeles doesn't even cost six figures, so I don't know how cardboard walls could cost six figures. Like. No, that was not six figures. I don't know how they spent that."

The Kamala camp also paid Beyoncé $10 million (again, she's worth $800 million) to appear at a rally in Houston, when many who attended were majorly pissed-off after the singer didn't, you know . . . actually perform. Instead, $10 million bought the Harris team a four-minute speech by Beyoncé that nobody remembers outside of her *not* singing "Crazy in Love."

The hits kept coming, all thanks to Obama-ites Steph Cutter, Jen O'Malley Dillon, and David Plouffe, who took over the campaign from the Biden team. Cutter led this effort with Plouffe's approval to get low-propensity voters out for Kamala, having forgotten that Hillary had deployed the same ridiculous strategy back in 2016. Look at these bribes, er, payouts:

- $5 million for someone who calls themself Megan Thee Stallion
- $3 million for Lizzo
- Nearly $2 million for Eminem

Plouffe and Cutter ran Obama's campaigns more than a decade ago but haven't done much on the campaign front since. They tried to apply an outdated 2012 model to the 2024 election, forgetting that Kamala Harris is certainly not Barack Obama on the campaign trail and that celebrities genuinely embraced Obama. Harris was profoundly unpopular even in California, dating back to the last time she ran for president in 2019.

How could these strategists possibly think that bribing celebrities to appear to Kamala rallies in order to give the illusion that her support was real wasn't seen for what it was? How could they believe that having millionaire performers lecture voters in states like Wisconsin, Michigan, Pennsylvania, and Georgia would sway the kind of male, Black, Latino, and working-class voters they needed to win?

Look at the coverage of Taylor Swift's endorsement of Kamala Harris. Actual news organizations clearly didn't learn a thing, because an overwhelming number of voters do not change or make their vote based on what a singer tells them.

ABC News featured the headline "How Taylor Swift's Endorsement Could Shape the 2024 Election." More: "It's not just young people Swift is in a position to sway. Many of her fans belong to another critical demographic: white women, over half of whom voted red in both 2016 and 2020," the report reads.

"It's a huge voter block—and not only that, but it's a voter block that we've seen be consequential with regards to elections, particularly with Donald Trump," explained the one "expert" ABC interviewed for the story, University of Michigan professor Marcus Collins.

"How Swift's endorsement will shape the election is yet to be seen," the report concludes. "But her message's reach has already been massive."

Yes. *Massive.* So massive that in a related story, Trump won 52 percent of white women voters, helping to fuel his landslide.

"The truth is this is just an epic disaster, this is a one-billion-dollar disaster," an irate Linda Li, now-formerly of the Democratic National Committee's finance committee, vented to Will Cain on *Fox & Friends Weekend* days after the election.

"They're twenty million dollars million in debt. It's incredible, and I raised millions of that. I have friends I have to be accountable to and explain what happened because I told them it was a margin-of-error race," she added in the same interview, dropping an F-bomb on national television.

"I was promised . . . Jen O'Malley Dillon promised all of us that

Harris would win," she also shared. "She even put videos out saying that Harris would win. I believed her, my donors believed her, and so they wrote massive checks. I feel like a lot of us were misled."

Because they were. Jordan Belfort, the real-life *Wolf of Wall Street*, compared the campaign to a Ponzi scheme on *Jesse Watters Primetime*.

By the way, what does this campaign spending say about Kamala Harris and her team's ability to run the U.S. economy or government efficiently? This was a preview, and based on this example alone, thank God a Harris-Walz administration never came to fruition.

Here are two more big reasons why we should all be thankful the Coconut Queen isn't running the economy. Biden-Harris spent $7.5 billion on EV charging stations. Do you know how many charging stations were produced in their administration? Just thirty-seven. That's approximately $202 million per charging station.

They, along with Democrats in Congress, also spent $42.5 billion on rural internet service. Do you know how many have been connected? Not. One.

As for Trump the Sequel, he now has the House, Senate, and the Oval in his second term. But those in charge (Mike Johnson as House Speaker and John Thune as Senate majority leader) are far more aligned with Trump's vision than Paul Ryan and Mitch McConnell were in 2017, so without Covid there to blow up budgets, Trump should further rein in spending as well.

The Harris campaign spending itself out of existence is no surprise in retrospect.

In Trump 2.0, cabinet members and aides loyal to MAGA won't run to the press to sabotage his presidency the way some of his people did eight years ago.

The Trump Interview

The thing about Donald Trump that his critics—the ones who called him a fascist/racist/xenophobe/Hitler will never accept is that he's one of the most affable, personable, dare I say, charming public figures you'll ever be around.

This December 2024 morning when I interviewed him for this book was no exception. His mood was downright jovial.

"Thank you for taking the time this morning, Mr. President. Appreciate it," I said to start the conversation.

"Hey, Joe! The book looks good, huh? That's a great cover. You know, I got a call from the Google people. It was the first time I heard from them in a long time. And they said that the McDonald's photo, the one you used [for the cover] had the largest number of views in the history of Google. It broke the bank. I said, 'What about the garbage truck [photo]?' They said, 'Far less. Not even close.' So you know what you're doing, Joe."

The cover photo has received tons of praise, I have to admit. My elbow hurts from patting myself on the back so much.

I then asked Trump what kept him moving forward despite all of these efforts to sideline him, jail him, even kill him. Lesser individuals, especially those with his kind of money and power, would have thrown in the towel and enjoyed the good life. With Trump, it always felt like a fixed fight against him. Impeachments, lawfare, media hostility, assassination attempts. But he just keeps moving forward. Why?

"Well, first of all, you have to understand your opponent. They're sick and very delusional. We've never seen anything like it," he replied before pivoting to what Democrats were doing before he took office by selling off his border wall panels for pennies on the dollar out of spite.

"They want to get five cents, even three cents on the dollar for very expensive wall panels that were designed specifically for this project. Hardened steel, hardened concrete and rebar, all put together and exactly what the border patrol wants. Selling it for pennies on the dollar, knowing that in a matter of weeks, it will be put up where it should be. And knowing also that to reorder it, it will cost at least three times more than what it did five years ago because of inflation and steel prices, you're talking about hundreds of millions of dollars being wasted. They really want to sell it for scrap metal because they want to hurt our country.

"Just another one," he continued. "We want people [federal employees] to show up for work. And they're giving forty-eight thousand people in D.C. the right not to come to work for five years. These are sick people.

"But one of the main reasons I did this [run again], you look at the numbers, the fifty-one intelligence agents, who all lied. The most recent election proved that obviously that the election was wrong in 2020. So if I thought if I came even close to losing that election, I wouldn't have run again. But I know how well we did. We had such a great election in 2020. It was such a shame what happened. We have to make sure we have honest elections in this country. We need strong borders and we need honest elections, Joe."

I switched to something I've wanted to talk to him about more than anything else: The first assassination attempt. What was he thinking when it first happened and why did he stand up and pump his fist when he still could be at risk?

"Well, I felt the bullets going over my head. I was so lucky I went down so fast," he recalled. "Actually, the Secret Service was very brave because, you know it's a different [Secret Service] group that handles the location of assets. But the guys who were with me were on top of me very immediately. You hear the bullets—I never thought I'd ever be hearing this sound—but they go whizzing by. But it had stopped. There was one different-sounding bullet that was the sniper, our sniper, who was amazing to hit him from that far away.

"So I didn't feel that. I didn't think about that actually [other shooters]. I had assumed it stopped. Because there was a lot of activity as you can imagine. I also had a very strong awareness of what had happened to me. The Secret Service, because of the amount of blood, thought I was hit in numerous locations, because there were many bullets fired. I said nope, I was hit in the ear. I was hit in the ear. You know, when I went to the White House [after winning in 2016], I stood in front of the Lincoln Bedroom, that was a surreal experience to me.

"But when I was hit, I was totally aware of what was happening," he noted. "It was strange. I knew I was bleeding a lot. Don't try it, Joe, but when you get hit in the ear, it bleeds more than from other places because of cartilage. So I wanted to get up, because I thought it was a bad, bad signal to stay down. I also knew that as long as I stayed down, people are going to assume I was no longer around. You know, you have a family. I had my family watching it on television. My wife was watching. And my son, [Barron,] ran in, a young boy had told him, 'Your father has been shot,' I mean, can you imagine my kid? He was very upset. So I felt I had to get up."

Then he shared a notable tidbit I hadn't heard about before.

"They had a stretcher next to me. They wanted me to go on the stretcher. There was no way I was going on a stretcher."

No, there wasn't . . .

It was revealed by the Harris campaign after the election that they never had any polling numbers internally showing they were leading. Any public pronouncements before November 5 that "late deciders" were breaking for Kamala was all bullshit to raise more money. But on Trump's end, he had two of the best pollsters in the business, John McLaughlin and Tony Fabrizio. And Trump trusted them both given their track records.

"We had very good numbers. Fabrizio and McLaughlin had us leading it pretty easily. My only fear was cheating. If we could keep the cheating down to a minimum. They cheat like broken dogs. They're still counting votes in California," Trump said. [Author's note: This interview took place in December 2024.]

"When you go to a normal state, you walk in, they check your records, they check your documentation. It's really hard to cheat. When you do mail-ins stuff, it means automatically they're going to state. Did you hear I won every state where there was verification? Every state. Our elections are totally corrupt."

"Can you change that when you get in?" I asked.

"We're going to try. We're going to work with Mike Johnson. But it's embedded. And they will fight you to the death. Look at California. You get arrested if you ask someone for voter ID," he correctly noted. And in a related story, the only states Kamala Harris won had weak voting requirements, including not requiring voter ID.

When Donald Trump won in 2016, he was dealt a similar hand: Republican control of Congress and Senate. But his first year in office was mostly in tumult. His effort, for example, to repeal and replace Obamacare was defeated in the Senate, all thanks to Mitch McConnell's limp support and the late Senator John McCain voting against the measure out of spite.

So what would be different this time around?

"There's a couple of differences between this win and the first win. I'm getting much more cooperation from the biggest players. You see them coming for dinners and everything else. They fought me for four years and this one they didn't. One [difference] was the size of the victory. Winning the popular vote was a big deal. You know I won it by a lot. And I say that despite California, because that vote is really crooked. It's out of control. And also won the electoral vote by a lot."

This is true. Trump was called a Russian agent entering office the first time around. He was called illegitimate by the media and his opponent. And not winning the popular vote made the victory not feel totally complete because it gave his critics a "He won, *but . . .*" argument. Winning the popular vote in 2024 was something few believed could happen, making his mandate that much stronger in 2025.

On another front, did I tell you my son is a smart kid? So, on the morning of the interview, I asked him what I should ask the future president. Note: My daughter is on safety patrol at her elementary school and had already left, since she needs to be there earlier, hence no question from her.

Liam's question. He's nine years old.

"Can you ask him how he's going to bring down the price of cheeseburgers?"

It's a good question. My kids are allowed to have McDonald's once a month. Admittedly, the McDonald's documentary by the late Morgan Spurlock, *Super Size Me*, scared me straight. So we try to limit the McDonald's runs to monthly. But when we do go, Liam is right: Even McDonald's has become expensive (he based his perspective on my complaints upon paying every time).

As for Trump, his perspective on lowering the cost of fast food was one I hadn't heard before.

"Well, it's all about the energy," he responded after chuckling about the question. "The energy is the big baby. If that comes down, then the trucks that go out serve various restaurants, McDonald's, all of them. But the gasoline's lower. The costs are lower. The heating's lower. The ovens cost you less. Everything is going to come down. Energy will bring down the interest rates.

"So you tell him, we're going to get the energy way down. And when the energy comes down, it's going to lower the cost of everything, including his [chuckles again] cheeseburgers."

Trump may be in his late seventies, but he still has a teenage son, the aforementioned Barron. As Karoline Leavitt shared earlier in the book, Trump is an exceptional listener. He solicits opinions from a wide array of people. That included Barron when it came to media strategy.

"He's at an age where he sees things that we don't see as much," Trump explained. "He was giving me some names that I had never heard of. Of course, I had heard of Joe Rogan, and we were talking to Joe Rogan about doing something. But that turned out to be a great interview. That was great, wasn't it? I just spoke to [Rogan]. He says he had 212 million views for that one."

For context, the entire population of Russia is 145 million.

Of course, I also had to ask about the Al Smith dinner, which marked the biggest unforced error of the campaign for the Coconut Queen.

"Maybe you or I would understand it maybe better than [Kamala] because she's not a New Yorker. The Al Smith dinner is a big deal. Very big in New York and very big for the Catholic church. They raise millions and millions of dollars," Trump said. "I've gone to it many times and I've participated in it. And I had a good night that night, they say, I just read the reviews. It's not easy doing comedy, even for comedians. Even the best ones bomb. It was on television all over the place. It has a tremendous audience. They raised a lot of money and she didn't show up.

"Not only that, she did a tape that was very short and it was totally inappropriate. It was crazy," he added. "It was worse than her not showing up because the tape was horrible. I couldn't believe it when I saw it. She made a mistake. She should have shown up. Same thing with Joe Rogan. It was obvious she should have done it. Mine, by that time, was done. She should have done a counter. But she didn't do it. Maybe she thought she couldn't do it."

The conversation turned to JD Vance. I asked if his vice-presidential pick exceeded even his high expectations.

"Yeah. By about two hundred percent," Trump deadpanned. "I thought he'd be good. I knew he was very smart. I really got him for the brain power because he really is a smart guy.

"But what I didn't know, the personality, he's a very solid person with a good personality. They really went after him that first week, and we were able to quell that fake story. And that's been it. He did great in the debate. This opponent [Tim Walz] was so inappropriately picked. We felt we were very lucky when they picked Walz. He was terrible. I don't even know how you get a worse person.

"Now, I'm no fan of Shapiro," he continued, "but I think they would have at least had a shot with Shapiro. I've been watching Shapiro more lately, and I'm not a big fan. I don't get it. At least they maybe would have a shot in Pennsylvania. But I don't think so. I think we would have won Pennsylvania anyway. Any chance they had was dissipated the night she picked this Walz. He was terrible. With that being said, vice presidents don't win you the election, it just doesn't seem to be that way historically."

Some other questions:

Q: "Do you think Joe and Jill Biden voted for you?"
A: "That's funny. I think they were not as unhappy [about Kamala losing] as you would normally think."

A question from my eighty-two-year-old father. Figured I'd spread the questions wealth a bit . . .

"Just how personally proud and vindicated are you by your land-slide victory and the acceptance of the general public as to the country's future under your direction are you?"

"Really, there are no words. It's incredible what has happened," he replied. "And part of it is how bad they've been. Joe, the fact is that people have seen four years of horror. Four years of broken borders. Energy prices that went through the roof. Interest rates that are too high. And crime at levels never seen before. People saw that and I think that made a tremendous difference.

"I actually think the four years [of Biden-Harris] was important," he concluded, "Because it showed how bad they were. And they don't want to change. But I do see they're back on their hind feet. They were much more enthusiastic four years ago after the election in trying to destroy the country. They've totally lost their confidence."

And finally, from me:

"Looking back on this campaign, what do you feel the most proud of?"

"There has never been a great group of people like MAGA. There's never been a movement like this, Joe," he described, almost in awe. "That's why you're writing the book. You've seen it. There's never been anything like it, and there probably won't be anything like it in the future. And MAGA is now going to do the work. It's one thing to win an election, now we have to produce.

"And we will."

EPILOGUE

In a weird way—and hear me out on this—it's almost better that Donald Trump won in 2024 than 2020.

Think about it strictly from a political perspective. Let's say Covid ended up never emerging from that lab in Wuhan, China. Let's say Donald Trump, powered by peace and prosperity, beat Joe Biden in 2020 the same way we beat Kamala Harris: soundly. And he *would have* in a normal election. What would be awaiting him in 2021?

Answer: a Democrat-controlled House and Senate hungry for some more toothless impeachments and stopping the president at every turn. Trump's agenda would have been hamstrung during such a second term. Gridlock would have ruled the day. And by the time 2023 would have come along, we would already have been talking about who the front-runners in the presidential race were on both sides, with Trump term-limited.

I go back to that Wildwood, New Jersey, rally in May 2024, when Trump talked about the MAGA movement having more passion and energy behind it than ever before. He spoke about Americans getting four years of the alternative that included massive spending, lots of time at the beach for the president, more war, more crime, millions of more illegals, and basically everything being more expensive. The alternative, of course, was Biden-Harris. And this wasn't just bravado from Trump: the numbers backed it up. Right before that Wildwood rally, CNN released a poll that showed 55 percent of voters saying they considered Trump's presidency a success. That was up from 41 percent in the same poll taken in January 2021, marking a 14-point jump. Simply put, the alternative from early 2021 to early 2025 prompted a considerable amount of people, even Democrats, to appreciate the Trump years in his first term. The 2024 election reflected that in spades.

I spoke to Karoline Leavitt, Trump's campaign press secretary at the time, shortly after the election and asked her the one thing about Donald Trump that people may not know about him.

"He listens," she told me in a radio interview on 710-WOR in New York. "He values the opinions of everyone around him. And oftentimes he'll come to you and say, 'What do you think about this?'"

At just age twenty-seven, Karoline would go on to become the youngest White House press secretary in history.

That listening aspect marked a key moment for the campaign when Rob Gleason, the former chair of the Pennsylvania Republican Party, convinced Trump to embrace early voting with a masterly argument in April during a meeting arranged by Trump campaign senior adviser (and current chief of staff Susie Wiles) and then RNC co-chair Lara Trump, who both strongly supported early voting.

"Sir, your people are so excited to vote for you that they want to as soon as they can," Gleason told Trump, according to *Time* magazine. "They don't want to wait. But you gotta tell them it's okay. You gotta give them permission."

Trump differed from his 2016 and 2020 stances and pushed hard on early voting. It clearly paid off, with early voting records being broken in states like North Carolina and Georgia. Trump built sizable leads in Arizona and Nevada before the election, meaning Democrats would have to outperform Republicans on election day, which never happens.

I saw the early totals coming in and couldn't help myself during a late-October appearance on *Hannity*.

"He wins this quite easily. Save the tape. Play it back if I'm wrong. This is how it's going to end," I predicted. And on cue, the morons at Media Matters whipped up a piece called "The right is projecting irrational confidence about a Trump win. That could aid an effort to steal the election."

How's that looking now, fellas?

So what will be different moving forward? Experience. Trump didn't know Washington when he entered office in 2017. He may not have fully appreciated—and few of us could have at the time—that Democrats would go to the extremes they would with the impeachments, the lawfare, the weaponization of so many aspects of government, and the "threat to democracy" rhetoric that drove Ryan Routh to nearly assassinate Trump from the sniper's nest outside the sixth hole at Trump International. It all turned out to be quite real.

Trump 2.0 is *more* than ready for this, hence his cabinet selections, in which many of the people who were nominated were victims of the very entities they will now be running if confirmed. (Author's note: This book went to press as Trump was taking office, hence the "if confirmed" disclaimer.)

According to the Brookings Institution, Trump's senior executive staff turnover reached 92 percent by the end of his first term. Granted, when you were once the star of a show that centered on firing people, this ain't surprising.

In contrast, Biden fired nobody of significance in his first term.

What's that? You completely botched the Afghanistan withdrawal? Let's have lunch!

You allowed a twenty-year-old with a rifle and scope to outflank the entire Secret Service to get a perfect line of sight on Trump at a rally? Oh well.

Inflation just went past 9 percent? You're doing a helluva job!

Oh, the border's a catastrophe? Don't worry, Mayorkas, you're not going anywhere.

Maybe it's just me, but I'd rather have a president who holds people accountable than one who lets everyone skate.

All of that being said, Trump's second term should see far less turnover than the first, only because he has a team around him that is completely in sync with his agenda and worldview. Almost all on board were loyal throughout the campaign and actually *want* to work with him to make the country and the world a better place. The first time around, especially in 2017, the team around him seemed more about pushing their own agendas while leaking to the press on an hourly basis as part of a circular firing squad.

In Trump 2.0, Elon Musk and Vivek Ramaswamy will be running DOGE (Department of Government Efficiency), for example, which is going to massively trim the fat of the government. Vivek wants 75 percent of it cut, while Elon cut 80 percent of Twitter staff with the site only to be more efficient during the Musk era. That's something we didn't see in Trump, Act 1: a real focus on cutting waste and spending by two people willing to do so without apology.

Trump's attorney general, Pam Bondi, will be a huge upgrade from Trump's first AG, Jeff Sessions, who handed Democrats an easy win by recusing himself from the Russia investigation. Would Eric Holder or Merrick Garland have ever done such a thing to their wingmen? Not on your life.

Susie Wiles will be Trump's chief of staff, which is significant because she, along with Chris LaCivita, truly had the president's ear in steering a successful campaign that outworked and outsmarted Team Kamala at every turn.

Doug Burgum, as secretary of the interior, is also a fine pick, given his experience in the energy sector. If there is one guy who likes to drill, baby, drill as much as Trump, it's the former North Dakota governor. Gas prices and home heating prices will be noticeably lower by the end of 2025, barring some catastrophic event. Save the prediction.

Kash Patel, who will run the FBI if confirmed, is an example of someone victimized by a government entity only to later run it, as is Robert F. Kennedy Jr. at the Department of Health and Human Services, who was villainized by the left for the crime of pushing for safer vaccines and healthier food for our children in a country where obesity is a national scourge.

Linda McMahon is on the same page as Trump at the Department of Education in her agreement to dismantle it and send decisions about educating our children back to the states and local boards, where they belong. Tom Homan, as border czar, will undoubtedly secure the border and successfully battle blue governors and mayors who won't help deport those here illegally, especially criminal gangs.

There are so many more solid cabinet and noncabinet picks, including my friends from Fox (Pete Hegseth at Defense, Sean Duffy at Transportation, Dr. Janette Nesheiwat for surgeon general, and Dr. Marty Makary at the Food and Drug Administration), but we'll wrap a bow around this theme here with one common thread: all of these picks have shown commitment to Trump and the MAGA agenda through all the ups and downs. It's a cabinet of diversity in terms of party and background, and it's also on the relatively younger side, but they will need all the energy in the world to keep up with the tireless Trump, who, as I was told by one of his close aides, Natalie Harp, following a stretch when Trump did five rallies in thirty-six hours, doesn't even drink coffee (I personally wouldn't survive without it).

If Trump and his team can accomplish these ten goals alone, he will go down as one of the greatest presidents ever in the eyes of the American people. They are:

1. Lower inflation to below Trump's first-term levels of below 2 percent.

2. Extend the Trump tax cuts *and* institute no tax on tips, no tax on overtime, and no tax on Social Security. Lower the corporate tax rate from 21 percent to 15 percent.

3. Make America Safe Again by pressuring rogue liberal DAs to enforce the laws on the books while offering financial incentives to increase police recruitment.

4. Secure the border with the help of Mexico and Canada

through threats of tariffs. Finish the wall with the help of Congress. Reinstitute Remain in Mexico. End catch-and-release.

5. Begin mass deportation with the first phase of arresting and deporting all illegals with criminal records out of the country.

6. Reduce federal spending based on recommendations from DOGE by $2 trillion from the annual budget.

7. End wars in Gaza and Ukraine through Reagan's "Peace Through Strength" model.

8. Dismantle the U.S. Department of Education while offering school-choice tax breaks for parents.

9. Lower gas prices via "drill, baby, drill" while becoming energy-independent again.

10. Make sure voter ID is required in all fifty states.

Honorable mention: Make it federal law to not allow sex changes from any minors under eighteen without parental consent. And do not allow biological men to compete against biological women in sports, nationwide.

Think of the kind of country the United States would be compared to now if these goals were met. Then think about what Democrats could possibly run on in 2028 if Trump is as successful as many believe he will be.

As for Dems, they certainly cannot run on the "No one is above the law" crap anymore, all thanks to Joe Biden's December 2024 pardon of his son Hunter, which dated back to 2014 to cover not only any and all crimes and misdeeds Hunter participated in, but ones his father played an active role in facilitating. Biden had promised repeatedly he wouldn't issue such a pardon, but to no one's surprise (because he's a pathological liar), he did it anyway.

Joe Biden, as I wrote in my 2022 book on his life, has always been about two things: his own power and enriching the family. That's it. The blanket pardon of Hunter proved it. He doesn't care about or respect our institutions. He never wanted to unify the country. And, yes, his administration was clearly pulling the strings on the Trump trials given that the number three guy in Biden's Justice Department, Michael Colangelo, suddenly decided to leave that post and join Manhattan district attorney Alvin Bragg's team in their fight against Trump. This was somehow a career upgrade.

Biden left office with one of the lowest approval ratings in polling history for an outgoing president. After the election, more Democrats came out publicly to fume that he didn't drop out of the race much earlier (which was beyond rich since, these were the same people telling us Biden was sharp as a tack). And that Hunter pardon? It finally changed the perception of him by gullible members of the party that maybe he wasn't the second coming of George Washington after all.

"Now everyone looks stupid. Everyone looks like they are full of shit," declared Tommy Vietor of the Obama bros' patently pious *Pod Save America* podcast. "And Republicans are going to use this to argue it was politics as usual when Democrats warned of Trump's corruption or threat to the rule or the threat to democracy. And I think that's the piece of this I am most frustrated with, which is Joe Biden looking like a typical, lying politician. And I think that leads to a cynical feeling that all politicians are bad. They are all the same, and that this is just par for the course."

Don't expect our media to have the same Come-to-Jesus moment like Tommy Vietor. Just check out these two headlines on Trump pardons in 2020 compared to Biden in 2024 from the same publication, the *New York Times*.

Trump in December 2020:

President Trump doled out clemency to a new group of loy-
alists on Wednesday, wiping away convictions and sentences
as he aggressively employed his power to override courts,
juries and prosecutors to apply his own standard of justice
for his allies. One recipient of a pardon was a family member,
Charles Kushner, the father of his son-in-law, Jared Kushner....
The president has long publicly dangled the prospect of pardons for associates caught up in investigations in a way that
critics argued amounted to a bid to convince them to keep
quiet about any wrongdoing they may have witnessed by
Mr. Trump.

Biden in December 2024, same paper:

A dark sky had fallen over Nantucket, Mass., on Saturday evening when President Biden left church alongside his family
after his final Thanksgiving as president. Inside a borrowed
vacation compound earlier in the week, with its views of the
Nantucket Harbor, Mr. Biden had met with his wife, Jill Biden,
and his son Hunter Biden to discuss a decision that had tor-
mented him for months. The issue: a pardon that would clear
Hunter of years of legal trouble, something the president had
repeatedly insisted he would not do. . . . It was at that point
Mr. Biden, who was, among other things, deeply concerned
that the pressure of the trials would push his son into a relapse
after years of sobriety, began to realize there might not be any
way out beyond issuing a pardon.

You can't make this stuff up. It's the death of shame, as my pal
Jimmy Failla likes to say. Our media will *never* learn. Teaching an old
dog new tricks is one thing. Teaching corrupt old dogs new tricks is an
even more insurmountable task.

And no book about Trump Derangement Syndrome would be

complete without Ana Navarro, who somehow gets paid nice money by *two* networks to offer up analysis like this on the Hunter pardon.

"Woodrow Wilson pardoned his brother-in-law, Hunter deButts. Bill Clinton pardoned his brother, Roger. Donald Trump pardoned his daughter's father-in-law, Charlie Kushner. And just appointed him Ambassador to France. But tell me again how Joe Biden 'is setting precedent'?" she wrote on X.

Hmmm. . . . *Hunter deButts*. That name seems both ironic and out of place here, doncha think? Ana never picked up on the fact that her fact-check might not be correct. I mean, you half expected her to also argue that Amanda Huggenkiss was pardoned by Gerald Ford.

Turns out there never *was* a Hunter deButts pardoned by Woodrow Wilson. Navarro, who can never admit ever being wrong on CNN or ABC's *The View*, blamed (checks notes) ChatGPT.

"Hey Twitter sleuths, thanks for taking the time to provide context. Take it up with ChatGPT," she wrote, complete with laughing emojis.

Yep. She asked ChatGPT about presidential pardons of the past instead of doing a simple Google search herself.

There are no words.

The truth is that, ultimately, Democrats don't seem to believe in anything outside of unlimited abortion on demand. Remember "My body, my choice"? That slogan seemed to go out the window once Covid came along. People were *fired* over not taking the jab; others were ostracized and shamed. Instead the slogan became "Your body, *our* choice."

Dems believe in war now. They hate the First Amendment. And the Second Amendment. But they love Lawfare. And really love court-packing, but only if they're the ones in power. Their base are hedge fund billionaires, celebrities, and single women. That's fine, but winning national elections is going to be difficult moving forward if that's the coalition.

But what if Trump had decided to sit out 2016? What if Hillary Clinton had defeated, say, Jeb Bush in the general election? The result would have been a 6–3 liberal Supreme Court, voting laws changed to benefit Democrats, including no voter ID, fifty-two states to give Dems a permanent majority in the Senate, and the end of the filibuster. The country and the world would be a completely different place. Republicans would be banished perhaps permanently.

Donald Trump can make our country and the world a completely different place by 2028. If successful over the next four years, the Blue Team could be reduced to the JV for the foreseeable future. That's how consequential the 2024 election was. Because if he lost, one could only imagine the nightmare that would have Kamala Harris and Tim Walz (and whoever controlled them behind the scenes) running the country.

Instead, America has hope. A postelection poll by Echelon Insights found that by a 20-point margin, Americans feel 2025 will start to head in a better direction (58 percent to 38 percent, with 4 percent not sure). And by a 2-to-1 margin, they feel their finances will be better after four more years of Trump, with just 18 percent believing they'll be worse off financially (YouGov).

At Trump's inauguration speech, which was held inside the Capitol Rotunda due to dangerously cold weather, Trump called the Republic's next chapter the "Golden Age of America" while reassuring the country that "America's decline is over." And he did so with Joe Biden and Kamala Harris right behind him, having to take it all in. They both mostly looked down at their shoes. Fitting.

To quote one of the last lines in my favorite movie of all time, *The Shawshank Redemption*, "Hope is a good thing, maybe the best of things, and no good thing ever dies."

That's the American spirit. And after witnessing the comeback of Donald J. Trump, arguably the most improbable comeback we have seen since the Revolutionary War, we are a hopeful country again.

Normalcy won.

We can be great.

Again.

Thanks for reading.

ACKNOWLEDGMENTS

Needless to say, I'm a lucky guy. I have two wonderful kids, Liam and Cameron, who always put a smile on my face while making Daddy proud. And a wife who is the best thing that ever happened to me. I would also like to thank the folks at Fox News and HarperCollins for their continued support of my career not just on TV but with my writing in both columns and books. No better company to work for. To my editors, Hannah Long and Eric Nelson, for their tireless work in turning this book around so quickly. If you're happy in work and family and life, that's the ultimate trifecta.

ABOUT THE AUTHOR

Joe Concha is a Fox News contributor and the author of two bestsellers this decade: *Come On, Man! The Truth About Joe Biden's Terrible, Horrible, No-Good, Very Bad Presidency* and *Progressively Worse: Why Today's Democrats Ain't Your Daddy's Donkeys*.